Mr. Mayor

Mr. Mayor

by A. J. Cervantes
Two-Term Mayor of the City of St. Louis

with Lawrence G. Blochman

Foreword by Senator Hubert H. Humphery

Nash Publishing, Los Angeles

Library of Congress Catalog Card Number: 74-83035
International Standard Book Number: 0-8402-1350-6

Published simultaneously in the United States and Canada
by Nash Publishing Corporation, 9255 Sunset Boulevard
Los Angeles, California 90069

Printed in the United States of America

First Printing

A man who wishes to achieve success in life should have a wife who is not only understanding, but who is truly a partner. I have been fortunate to have had such a partner in Carmen; I have been able to share my joys, sorrows, achievements and disappointments with her—she is my greatest asset—and to her I dedicate this book.

ALFONSO J. CERVANTES

An acknowledgement to my good friend, Peter Simpson, for his contribution in the solving of many of the urban problems, for his aid, his advice and consultation in the writing of *Mister Mayor*.

Alfonso J. Cervantes

Contents

Foreword
by Senator Hubert H. Humphrey

This book by A. J. Cervantes is an important contribution toward a resolution of what he calls "the urban mess."

I can say this objectively despite the fact that Al Cervantes is a good friend of mine, for our relationship is rooted in my association with him as mayor of St. Louis. While I was taking hold of my duties as Lyndon Johnson's vice-president—with special responsibilities for dealing with the problems of our great cities—A. J. Cervantes was getting a foothold in the mayor's office.

We got to know each other well back in June of 1965 at the annual meeting of the United States Conference of Mayors. Although he had been in office less than two months, Al Cervantes had to act as host to that august gathering. Through tireless effort and attention to the smallest detail, he spearheaded a civic program that sent all the mayors home talking about what a warm, hospitable city Saint Louis was.

My days as mayor of Minneapolis were in the forefront of my mind as I went to assure all the chief executives of the cities that the administration in Washington was deeply concerned with the problems they were facing. As we talked, Al Cervantes lost no time in letting me know all the things his city was up against and in pressing me for a meaningful federal response to these needs.

That federal response, I regret to say, has been flickering badly in recent years and if the slaughter of social programs continues during the second Nixon administration, it is in real danger of practical extinction. So much has happened since the middle year of one of the most dynamic decades in the nation's history that it is sometimes difficult to tell from which direction the next challenge will come. Nowhere has the aftermath of those excruciating years been felt more intensely than in the cities. Every mayor in America has his own exciting, troubled story to tell, but few could tell it with the candor, flavor, and wit which Mayor Cervantes has brought to this book.

Moreover he has put his finger on the deep, underlying causes of much of the big city's woes. Failure of cooperation, he insists, between the various levels of government—city, state and federal—is largely to blame. Lack of understanding of local problems by the upper echelons of government, state, and suburbia have led to the fiscal inequities that have driven big cities to the edge of despair and the verge of bankruptcy.

Many things have been obscured during these dreary years, one of which was the cheerful, vibrant optimism which Americans have traditionally brought to all the difficulties that face them. It was good to find that this mayor, like so many of this strenuous breed, took arms against what at times seemed hopeless troubles with such a hopeful spirit.

Not only had the great urban issues camped on his doorstep at city hall, but also at the home he shared with his family. Yet he faced them, as this book relates, with a sharp, tough mind as well as an open, compassionate heart. The city of Saint Louis has been enriched by the years of service that Mayor Cervantes has given its citizens. Now the whole nation can share in the story of his trials, tribulations, and triumphs.

For anyone who wants to understand what urban affairs in America are all about (and that had better include all of us), this book should be required reading. When he closes its covers, he will realize why I am proud to call Al Cervantes my friend.

Hubert H. Humphrey
Washington, D.C.
July 1, 1973

Mr. Mayor

Introduction

The Urban Mess

There are some indications that this nation may wake up before the Great American Dream turns into the Great American Nightmare. As the coast-to-coast urban crisis becomes more critical day by day, as the gap widens between the bankrupt inner city and the affluent white suburbs, there are signs to indicate that we may be emerging from the civic and ethical apathy that survived even the turbulent sixties.

However, the fate of our cities and our urban civilization depends largely upon the answer to two questions:

Can our two now-hostile Americas, one rich, and one poor, one white and one black, attain a state of peaceful coexistence?

How will we make peace in the war for America's soul now being fought in the streets of our biggest cities, in our nation's capital, in the city halls and college campuses, and in the hearts and minds of Americans in all the 200-odd metropolitan areas across our disturbed land?

I believe the answer to the first question is a cautious and conditional yes.

My answer to the second question depends upon whether there can be a meeting of minds, wills, and pocketbooks at the three levels of government. I say categorically that at present American cities are being shortchanged. Petty jealousies and selfish interests at the state level, and nineteenth-century philosophy complicated by stupid bureaucratic stubbornness on the national plane, are well on the way to strangling our urban populations. Unless a fair share of the taxes paid by city dwellers is returned to the cities by state and national governments, the fate of the inner city is hopeless.

I believe, however, that the pages of this book will show that it is not too late to save the central cities. I believe that St. Louis is moving slowly in the right direction, even though St. Louis will probably soon join our four largest American cities which are already more than half black. When I first entered public life in 1949, Negroes made up only 18 percent of the city's population. When I was elected mayor in 1965 the percentage had grown to 36. At the end of my second term, the city had become more than 40 percent Afro-American. And our sister city East St. Louis, just across the Mississippi in Illinois, is nearly 70 percent black.

It is no secret that the influx of the impoverished and disadvantaged, mostly black, into our inner cities has been accompanied by an even greater outflow of well-heeled whites to the suburbs, leaving behind them decaying business blocks, boarded-up shop windows, thousands of jobless, and emaciated tax rolls. St. Louis had a net loss of 100,000 population between the 1960 and 1970 census despite an increase of 50,000 blacks. This has been the essence of our problem; this is the beanstalk we have had to climb—without any jack. And the national picture is just as dismal.

Why, then, do I allow myself a gleam of optimism when there is hardly a big city in the United States that is not in a similar predicament? Let me enumerate a few reasons:

—Because St. Louis is the epitome of mid-America, geographically, ethnically, and economically, and it may well be the pilot city in finding answers to seemingly impossible questions. We have learned by our own mistakes and the mistakes of others.

—Because we have had a number of experimental projects under way which may become key blueprints for the rehabilitation of other blighted core cities.

—Because we have had a modicum of cooperation between the races, a balance between militants and moderates of all complexions that has allowed St. Louis, of all major American cities, to go through the stormy 1960's free of the civil disorders that plagued nearly 300 other communities from Newark to Detroit to Watts.

—Because we have had a comprehensive, realistic program for civic revival which may serve as a prototype for other tax-starved, bureaucratically strangled, racially simmering cities. And because the program is of possible national interest I will give some details here.

The St. Louis master plan devised in the first year of my second term as mayor had been christened "The Challenge of the Seventies." To bring it into being, we recruited the best minds of the city to do a job of systems analysis on what was wrong with St. Louis, what actions were necessary to make essential improvement, establishing a priority for each recommendation and putting a dollar price tag on each project, so that as funds became available the top priorities would be first to be served.

As overall coordinator for the program, I asked C. Warren Reed to be general chairman. Mr. Reed is a partner in Ernst and Ernst, a firm with some 200 world-wide branches. An exceptional administrator in his own right, he has had access to the best analytical expertise available. Best of all, he was a Republican willing to serve a Democratic municipal administration to insure a nonpartisan approach to help stave off local and perhaps national disaster. His multiracial staff of eighteen chairmen were charged with evaluating and reweaving the political, social, economic, environmental, and physical fabric of the city of St. Louis—perhaps as an example for several hundred other bankrupt and bewildered American cities.

The eighteen functions of the body politic which our civic pathologists have been diagnosing, and for which they have already been prescribing therapy, include, in addition to the obvious categories of housing, crime prevention, education, transport, pollution and civil rights, such related fields as neighborhood organization, city beautification, and business development. People have been working in unison on these functions (with the usual human differences), and many have already been making scores.

When Neil Armstrong set the Eagle down on the Sea of Tranquility on July 20, 1969, he cut nearly six months off President John Kennedy's prediction that an American would walk on the moon by 1970. That fantastic feat was accomplished by teamwork—cooperation of government (NASA) and business expertise furnished by, among others, McDonnell-Douglas and several other St. Louis industrial necromancers. The same teamwork of government-with-government on various levels and of business-with-government, with the added factor of neighborhood and individual cooperation, hopefully will fulfill the prophecy of Pierre Laclède, the French fur trapper who founded the settlement near the confluence of the Mississippi and Missouri Rivers in 1763. On this site, Laclède is quoted as saying, as he looked out over the two great rivers flowing together from the heart of a continent, there should rise "one of the finest cities in America."

St. Louis is hard at work to meet the challenge, even if it has taken us two centuries to get started.

I

Decisions, Decisions.

No Hiding Place

When I entered public life shortly before my twenty-ninth birthday, anyone in his right mind, if asked to name the least likely character to serve as chief executive of the half-black city St. Louis was to become twenty years later, would have replied without hesitation: Alfonso J. Cervantes.

My conditioning had been all wrong for such a job. I was brought up to believe in a stable society where change was not only unthinkable but practically immoral. My Huck Finn-ish boyhood on the Mississippi down past the City Workhouse on South Broadway had taught me to accept the division of the world into two unequal parts—one black and one white—as natural, normal, and permanent.

We small fry would forage through alleys for abandoned milk and soda bottles we could turn in for the nickel deposits, and when we had enough capital we would rent a skiff—"johnboats" we called them—for fifty cents a day at some cruddy fishing shack on the river front. We would row out toward midstream to lie in wait for the great sternwheel excursion steamers to come churning by, throwing up huge rollers in their wake. Then we would work our oars furiously until we were close enough, dangerously close, to catch the thrilling rise and fall of the waves boiling up behind the paddle wheels, while whistles shrieked frantically and the captain bellowed at us from the bridge.

We saw nothing unusual in the fact that some sternwheelers like the *J.S.* were reserved primarily for white people while others like the *Saint Paul* carried primarily "colored folks."

Almost unbelievably, my boyhood attitude persisted during adolescence and the wanderings of my early adult years. I spent my late teens knocking about the country, riding the freights, sleeping in firehouses or hobo jungles, going respectable now and then to sell haberdashery or promote dance contests in the promotion capital of the world—Hollywood. During the Second World War, I was in the U.S. Merchant Marine, serving as radio officer on ships that ferried supplies and munitions over the seven seas, from the Aleutians to Australia and from Ceylon to Murmansk. Yet when I got back to my home town and settled down to a successful business career, I still saw society in terms of the *J.S.* and the *Saint Paul.* Moreover, I was a firm believer in the Puritan work ethic.

As I once wrote in the *Harvard Business Review,* I was firmly convinced that most of the world's problems would be solved if only everyone shared my faith in these simple principles:
- Poverty is the result of indolence; anyone who really wants a job can get one.
- The poor we will always have with us.
- Businessmen should commit themselves to making money, politicians to saving the cities, do-gooders to saving the disadvantaged, and preachers to saving souls.

This was my credo when I was first elected alderman from the Fifteenth Ward of South St. Louis, and in a way it explains my vote on the first controversial issue to come before the board of aldermen: the Public Accommodations Bill, which would open the city's bars, hotels, and eating places to patrons of all races.

I voted against it.

Looking back, I can see I was reflecting the mood of the city in the early fifties. People were trying to forget the grief and hardships of World War II. Young veterans like me were bent on catching up on years spent in the service, and their elders were too busy making money to be bothered with their neighbors' troubles.

There was no doubt that my vote against the bill represented the views of my middle-class white constituents, many of whom were descendants of highly individualistic Germans who fled Europe after the collapse of the 1848 revolutions. I agreed with them then that the owner of a bar, restaurant, or hotel had the right to choose the kind of customers he wanted. Most of the small taverns on the South Side were family affairs anyway. The average resident of the Fifteenth Ward considered the neighborhood saloon as his private club. He worked hard all day and felt he was entitled to relax with his kind at night and on weekends, just as he prayed with his kind at the neighborhood church every Sunday. He disliked change and he feared any possible invasion of his quiet tree-lined streets of solid, red-brick houses with their white front stoops and neat backyards.

My constituents of the Fifteenth Ward didn't think much of the lofty liberalism of the downtown civic leaders or the professional educators, both of whom probably lived in the opulent, lily-white suburbs anyway and didn't practice what they preached.

Only three of my fellow aldermen were Negroes, and two of them were Republicans. The black community, at that time not very numerous in St. Louis—about 18 percent—was unorganized and carried little political weight.

So I felt no compunction, political or moral, about voting against public accommodation.

My reeducation began immediately—with a bang!

First on the firing line was my elder brother, Lu, whom I have always admired and esteemed. The Reverend Lucius F. Cervantes, S. J., Ph.D., a scholarly sociologist and an eminent student of urban affairs, has always looked at sociology in terms of people rather than statistics. At the time he took me by the arm and sat me down to listen to what the Public Accommodations Bill meant in moral terms, the starch was scarcely dry on his Jesuit Roman collar.

Lu's eloquence convinced me that a man whose business was operating any form of public accommodations bore a public responsibility. He opened my eyes—long before the Kerner-Lindsay report pointed it out—to the increasing danger of discrimination and segregation to the nation; that no political structure could exist indefinitely with the separation of two societies widening; that the interests of the city as a whole were bigger than the provincial attitude of the Fifteenth Ward. I was greatly impressed by Lu's incisive mind and his deeply felt humanity. His arguments were unanswerable.

A little later I got a call from a voice I had not heard in years—that of Father Dismas Clark who had taught me freshman English at St. Louis University High School, and who had always had early doubts about the salvability of my soul. Father Dismas Clark later became famous as "the Hoodlum Priest" for his compassionate work of rehabilitation among convicts. His tough eloquence on behalf of the underdog had an overpowering public appeal, and I expected a thundering blast of invective when he identified himself. However, he sounded hurt rather than angry as he patiently explained why I was wrong in voting against public accommodation. He was surprised, he said in tones he usually reserved for wayward children, that I had made myself party to the dirty trick American life was playing on the black citizen. He worked on me until he made me feel I had been neglecting my duty to God and all mankind. He finished the job Lu had begun. I was a convert, but it was not going to be easy to explain my conversion to my constituents in the Fifteenth Ward.

When the bill came up next it failed again. This time, however, Alderman A. J. Cervantes voted "yea"—and got his first insight into the price to be paid for being on the right side of a controversy that still divided the city. My phone at home rang constantly for days, and when I picked it up I was sure to hear only vituperation and abuse. I was quite prepared to listen to the invective myself, for I understood the emotions aroused by the increasing influx of rural blacks into the aging parts of the city, but I was distressed by the thought of my wife Carmen answering in my absence and hearing people deplore her being married to a "nigger lover."

The cost of my vote was not merely personal and political, either. The vilification that came over the phone in the office of the Laclede Cab Company had dollar signs attached. The firm was in a critical stage of growth, for we were trying to compete with the established taxi fleets which thrived on family charge business. We were building up a call service with neighborhood bars and restaurants, and we needed the good will of bartenders and headwaiters—anyone a customer might ask to call a taxi. Our phone number had to be posted near public phones, for we had invested heavily in two-way radio equipment and we needed customers to pay for it.

The people to whom I was trying to sell insurance also let me know how they felt about interracial eating and drinking.

Despite continuing pressure from all sides, however, I stood my ground. My conversion was irreversible. And when the Public Accommodations Bill came before the board of aldermen for the third time, I campaigned actively for its passage, and that time it won.

My awareness of the differences between the levels of our society became more acute after I had become mayor. The contrast was brought out vividly and dramatically one spring evening in 1968 when we were giving a swank dinner party at our home in Westmoreland Place, a delightful bit of luxuriant suburbia practically in the heart of the city.

Westmoreland Place was particularly lush in spring when the tall, stately elms shading the private street were coming into leaf, the silvery dogwoods were budding, and the flowering shrubs were brightening the well-kept lawns of the expensive mansions. Carmen and I were very proud of our twenty-seven-room house there. In it, five years earlier when I was a candidate for president of the board of aldermen, Carmen had entertained on each of the twenty-eight days of February a group of women from each of the twenty-eight wards of the city, from the flossiest to the grubbiest. But the party on this particular spring evening was something else again. It was something special.

The guest list included the top names of the financial, industrial, and social elite of the city and county. They had contributed heavily to my project of bringing the Spanish Pavilion from the New York World's Fair to St. Louis, and they had been invited to meet Dr. Manual Fraga Iribarne, Spanish minister of tourism and information. His Excellency had come to St. Louis to decorate me with his government's Gold Medal for Touristic Merit.

I felt particularly proud that evening. While Carmen and I were dressing for dinner, a tureen of *gaspacho,* the national cold soup of Spain, stood chilling in the drawing room. Carmen had taken her menu from *The Embassy Cookbook,* a gift of the vivacious Marquesa Merry del Val, wife of the Spanish ambassador to the United States. The guests should begin arriving at eight.

I was not there to greet them.

I had scarcely finished dressing when I was called to the telephone. It was Bob Duffe, my chief of staff, with the bad news.

Dr. Martin Luther King had been shot dead in Memphis.

I was stunned by the shocking news and I could imagine its effect on our black community. I was going to have to find the words to express the city's grief at the loss of a great spiritual leader, words that I could hope might forestall any outbreak of violence in the ghetto in reaction to the senseless murder. Luckily my brother Lu arrived early. It was to be a sentimental evening for him, for he had studied with Dr. Fraga when the minister had been professor of political science at the University of Madrid. I immediately borrowed Lu's gift for words.

Bob Duffe had called the local radio and television stations and found they were setting up special programs. He sent Bill Jud to Westmoreland Place with the car and we made the rounds of the studios—KSD-TV, the NBC outlet; KMOX-TV, CBS; KTVI-TV, ABC; and KPLR-TV, a private station owned by my close friend Harold Koplar.

Everywhere I read the lines Lu had written:

All St. Louis is shocked and saddened by the tragic and violent death of Dr. Martin Luther King, a proponent of nonviolence. Violence and bloodshed will not solve but only complicate efforts to resolve civil rights problems. This is the time that effective and adequately supported programs to alleviate the problems of the disadvantaged must be pushed by all citizens of goodwill regardless of race, creed, or color. Violence, as evidenced in the fatal shooting of Dr. King, must be deplored by all who are committed to the proposition that all men are not only created equal but must have equal opportunities. With all St. Louis, my family and I are deeply grieved by the passing of this great leader and humanitarian who dedicated his life to social justice for all America.

As we rolled from station to station, I kept in touch with the police by radiophone. There were reports of disorders in various cities across the country, but the streets of St. Louis were quiet. Was it a stunned quiet, or the calm before the storm? I could only hope. . . .

An hour and a half had elapsed by the time we got back to Westmoreland Place. The tureen of gaspacho had been emptied and refilled many times. Carmen was moving through the groups of guests, seeing that the glasses were kept filled.

Everyone was good-natured and understanding about the delayed dinner when we finally entered the dining room. There was a sense of warmth generated, perhaps by the sympathy of our guests from overseas. I tried my best to be the genial host. Apparently I succeeded, but I was gripped by a cold feeling of premonition all evening.

After Dr. Fraga conferred the Spanish medal and presented Carmen with an exquisite antique fan of carved ivory and lace, I managed to make an appropriate speech of acknowledgment. But through it all I was listening with one ear for the telephone to ring. If trouble was erupting in other cities this night we might well expect demonstrations in St. Louis. The telephone was silent; so apparently were our streets.

It was after one o'clock when the last of the guests left and I could stretch out in a chair for a final drink before going to bed. Carmen and I were going over the highlights of the evening and had just come to the conclusion that the affair was a success when the phone finally rang.

It was Bill Bailey, an old friend of mine.

Bill Bailey was a black shipping clerk. He was only thirty-three years old, but he had nine kids. He was calling from the storefront offices of the Mid-City Community Congress at 4405 Delmar Boulevard on the shabby fringe of the ghetto.

"We're having a meeting here, Mr. Mayor," he said. "We're trying to make plans to do something to mark the death of Dr. Martin Luther King."

"A hell of a fine idea. I'll be right over," I said, not reflecting on the fact that I had not been invited.

It was two-thirty in the morning when I walked through the door of the storefront into the midst of a group of pained, angry, bitter black men and women. Their stares made me realize for the first time that I actually had not been invited. As mayor of the city, however, I still felt that it was fitting for me to be there.

The air was electric with hostility. Mayor or not, I had as little in common with these irate people as I did with the people I had entertained in my home a few hours earlier. My presence here was tolerated, but I was by no means a guest of honor. It was clear from the outset that everyone agreed with the militant voices that declared loudly and categorically that no white politicians were going to capitalize on the death of Dr. King. I, too, could agree to that.

Otherwise, there was very little agreement. A heated argument erupted between the NAACP's Morris Hatchett, a moderate—a Republican, in fact—and Jimmy Rollins, a determined and uncompromising militant. It was a no-holds-barred wrangle. The accumulation of frustration and resentment, repressed for centuries, was finding a voice tonight.

Finally the firm, quiet voice of Bill Bailey rose above the strident confusion and steered the meeting toward decisions that brought the black community together in its common sorrow. Bill Bailey had no organizational axe to grind. He had as little to gain from the dedication of the group as did a white politician. But he expressed the anguish and pain of the black community in the language of the soul brother. The depth and dignity of his grief captured the crowd.

It was apparent that I had only my presence to lend to the occasion. The wisest thing I could do was listen and learn. By the time I left at five in the morning I could testify that the black community of St. Louis was united as it never had been before.

This unity did much to keep peace in the difficult days that followed. More meetings and long discussions took place before final plans emerged. A few instances of fire-bombing flared in the interim but were quickly controlled.

The tribute to Dr. King was to be a march three days after his assassination. I declared the day, Sunday, April 7, 1968, to be one of citywide mourning. The crowd that assembled under the Gateway Arch early in the afternoon numbered only a few thousand, but the procession picked up tens of thousands more as it snaked through the ghetto on its eight-mile route. Thousands more lined the streets and sad faces pressed against windows as the marchers passed through the slums. The militants had accepted the role of marshals and kept order as the marchers moved along through the chilly spring sunlight.

It was an impressive, unforgettable spectacle—that packed, subdued mass of I don't know how many tens of thousands. Nobody claims to have come up with an accurate count, but I have never seen so large a group in quiet motion anywhere. The throng took four hours to walk the distance.

As I marched along with my brother Lu, Teamster Union leader Harold Gibbons, and Seventeenth Ward Alderman Joe Roddy, a white man with a racially mixed constituency, my mind was a million miles away from Dr. Fraga's medal and the distinguished gathering in West-moreland Place. I could think only of what Bill Bailey had said to me just before the march started: "Maybe I hate your guts, but I love Dr. King's so much that I'm willing to march with you today, even if I may fight with you tomorrow."

Paradoxically, my sympathy for the black cause, when it later came into conflict with my determination as mayor to try to run a solvent city, caused me to lose sleep over a political decision for the only time in my life. A bill declaring a city holiday for Dr. King's birthday came to my desk for signature after having passed the board of aldermen by a two-to-one vote. In view of my fiscal thinking at the time, the bill was definitely a hot potato, but I had only myself to blame for not being ready for it. My liaison with the board had obviously been faulty.

I had the deepest admiration for Dr. King's tremendous contribution toward a nonviolent correction of the inequity of our bi-racial society. I was genuinely grateful for the self-restraint of our black community in reacting to his senseless murder. While there were riots in 125 other cities in 29 states—President Johnson had to call on the army to restore order in Washington, D.C.—even the most militant of the black leader-ship in St. Louis joined in the inspired effort to keep the community cool.

In spite of all this, my first inclination was to veto the bill.

For weeks I had been wrestling with the dismal figures of the city budget. There was no escaping the fact that St. Louis was, to put it mildly, strapped. In my desperate search for more pennies to pinch, it occurred to me that we were not getting enough mileage out of our city employees. While several tenets of my Puritan ethic had been blown away by the winds of change, I still clung to the old-fashioned notion that an honest day's pay should produce an honest day's work.

Like most cities, St. Louis gives municipal employees some thirteen paid holidays a year beyond the usual vacation and sick leave. Adding all the workless days together, I was disturbed to get a total of about six weeks a year that city workers were drawing pay while not on the job. Given that the city's problems had reached almost insurmountable heights, adding still another holiday to the calendar went against my principles, no matter who was to be honored.

I found that my thinking hardly matched that of my peers during a meeting of the National Advisory Committee of the Democratic Party in 1968. Senator Fred Harris of Oklahoma was chairing a discussion of public apathy in elections. Vice-President Humphrey and Senator Muskie were sitting with Joseph Califano, general counsel for the Democratic National Committee. We were meeting at the Watergate in Washington—at that time, I believe, still free of electronic bugs and wiretaps—and debating ways of bringing more voters to the polls. Congressman Brooks of Beaumont, Texas, suggested combating widespread indifference by making election days a national holiday. Thus no voter would have a valid excuse for not exercising his franchise.

I got to my feet but restrained my gut reaction, which was anger. I didn't say, *Good Lord! Another day off? Don't we have enough laziness in this country?*

"Maybe I'm out of tune with the times," I began, "but I think the Democratic Party, as the party of the people, should encourage people to help build the country by working more productively, even if it takes more hours and fewer days off. I think the way to generate more interest in government is for our functionaries to set the example, to try to arouse enthusiasm for useful work, for tackling our problems head-on, not for seeking more leisure."

Thunderous silence greeted my remarks. Committee members exhcanged surprised, embarrassed glances. Finally Vice-President Humphrey got up.

"Al," he said, "I'm afraid you *are* out of tune with the times."

So it was my strong resentment of too many holidays that sparked my reluctance to sign the King birthday bill. To justify that resentment I had my staff analyze the cost to the city in lost work hours and compensatory time off. Translated into dollars the total quickly mounted to six figures—more than $200,000 worth of productive time that could have been used to ease some of the pains of urban malaise. Services desperately needed by many of the very people to whom Dr. King had devoted his life would be denied them if I signed the bill into law. A veto was logically indicated.

Because the fate of the King birthday bill was a potential time bomb in interracial relations, the press was most anxious to know what I was going to do. I kept holding them off, postponing the announcement of my final decision, which I was sure would arouse the ire of the black community. I had twenty days in which to sign or veto. If I did not sign in that time the bill became law without my signature. To skirt the issue in this way would deserve the contempt of both black and white communities. I let ten days go by without reaching a decision.

My staff came up with options which would honor Dr. King without costing the city a quarter of a million dollars. Why not make the Sunday following Dr. King's birthday the occasion for the holiday? No, that wouldn't work because the city charter guarantees employees the next Monday off when a holiday falls on Sunday. Then why not declare an official day of memorial for Dr. King, with all faiths holding services under the soaring Gateway Arch—but no time off for city employees. That might work, but I would have to veto the bill first. If I were sure the aldermen would sustain my veto . . . no, that would be shirking responsibility again. The decision must be mine alone.

On the eleventh day the impatient city hall reporters began asking ill-tempered questions. Why was I hesitating? Who or what was behind my uncharacteristic failure to make a quick decision? Was black militant pressure preventing me from using the veto?

That night I lay awake pondering a decision. I had to make up my mind by morning. I rehearsed all the pros and cons. My signature would cost the city nearly a quarter of a million dollars in lost time, and Mayor Cervantes the lost votes and goodwill of 100,000 conservative, insecure whites. My veto would be a slap in the face for the black community.

When Carmen brought my eye-opener that morning—my usual jug of prebreakfast coffee—my eyes had not even been closed. But I had made my choice. I had weighed civic dollars against people, and the people won. I couldn't get away from the nasty fact that blacks of our city had never got anything but the short end of the stick. They lacked a strong sense of pride, yet they had every reason to be proud of men such as Dr. King. One reason for their too-frequent absence of self-esteem was the tendency of their own militant leaders to sneer at those of their own people who had made a name in the white man's world. Booker T. Washington was ancient history. The portrait of George Washington Carver on a postage stamp was patronizing. The recognition of the late Jackie Robinson and Ralph Bunche as well as the appointment of Thurgood Marshall to the Supreme Court, was either tokenism or Uncle

Tomism. But an even greater reason was the eagerness of the white community to downgrade black achievements. The right of St. Louis blacks to bask in the glory of their champion Martin Luther King was worth more than a quarter of a million.

On the way to City Hall that morning I said to Bill Jud, my chauffeur, personal pilot, official photographer, and private ear-to-the-ground, "Bill I'm going to sign."

"Okay, Mr. Mayor," Bill Jud said as he stopped for a red traffic light, "but before you call in the reporters and the TV cameras, you'd better get in some extra telephone operators to handle all those boos and catcalls."

I brought in two extra operators.

There were exactly two angry calls of protest.

I did receive a small delegation of low-income whites from my old neighborhood of South St. Louis—waiters, porters, elevator operators— representing the basic resentment of those who felt most threatened by any improvement in the status of blacks. It was an angry group, but it was orderly and quite mild compared to some of the hornet swarms who have invaded city hall.

The rest of the official community followed my lead. The Board of Education closed the schools to honor Dr. King. The Catholic archdiocese did the same for the parochial schools. In making Martin Luther King's birthday a full-scale holiday, St. Louis seemed practically unanimous.

But not really.

In the Fifteenth Ward where I grew up, the men who had been the boys I used to play with along Juniata Street and on the fringes of Tower Grove Park proclaimed my name to be mud. Without a dissenting voice. And they expressed their sentiments a few years later at the polls. When I ran for the third-term nomination in 1973, the Fifteenth voted against me resoundingly.

But regardless of political or fiscal results of my decision, I felt the warming, inner satisfaction of having done the best thing for the city.

During my second term as mayor I had the further satisfaction of seeing material as well as moral benefits come the way of a disadvantaged minority—which meanwhile was inching closer to becoming a St. Louis majority.

II

It's a Long Way

Hollywood and the Road to Murmansk

Father Dismas Clark was not the only mentor of my youth who had misgivings about my ever growing up to amount to anything. The priests and nuns at St. Pius decided I was a menace to discipline in the lower grades and persuaded my mother that I might be happier elsewhere. Luckily Father Mulally of St. Mary Magdalen's, a school a few blocks farther west from our home, was willing to take a chance on me. He succeeded in turning my excess energy into less boisterous channels. I won a marbles championship in a tournament sponsored by the now-defunct *St. Louis Times.* I even studied enough to surprise everybody by getting through the eighth grade.

The graduation ceremonies were the occasion for my first lesson in practical politics: the art of compromise. Finishing the eighth grade meant more than just emerging from elementary school; it was a milestone that marked the entrance to adulthood, symbolized by getting rid of those hated knickers that only small boys wore. It meant wearing our first long pants.

Like all mothers, mine was reluctant to see the baby of the family grow up. She was dead set against long pants. After hours of pleading, however, I negotiated a compromise. Since my graduation suit would, for economic reasons, be a two-pants affair, it was agreed that we would get a pair of knickers to save face for Mama, and one pair of long pants to allow me a victory of principle.

Not only was my mother a strong-minded woman, but she was a person of great courage and determination. It was she who kept our family together after my father drifted away during the trying years of the Great Depression.

My father, Augustine A. Cervantes, was born in the Arsenal in South St. Louis where his father, who had come from Spain at the age of twelve, was quartermaster. My mother, née Victoria Kussenberger, was also a St. Louisan. She was born on South Broadway, the daughter of a house painter. The Kussenbergers had come from Alsace-Lorraine when it was German.

My parents met at the Lyons school when they were both students. My father became a meat inspector for the Department of Agriculture. Shortly after their marriage he was transferred to Port Townsend, Washington, where my oldest sister Catherine was born. Like a homing pigeon, he returned to St. Louis and resigned from government service. He had a great capacity for friendship, and taking advantage of all the contacts he had made among the meat-packers, he went into the insurance business.

He settled on the South Side, a few miles from his birthplace, and later moved to a solid, four-bedroom brick house at 3723 Juniata Street, where I was born. Although women were beginning to go to a hospital for delivery, my mother still didn't favor such impersonal, modern practices. With Grandmother Kussenberger standing by, I was born in the upstairs front room of that rented house on August 27, 1920. When I was old enough I joined the other kids who slept in the roomy attic.

When I started school I walked the eight blocks to St. Pius, although I could have taken the now-vanished trolley cars like the ones Judy Garland sang about in *Meet Me in St. Louis.* For us kids, streetcars were strictly for fun. After school we would steal rides by hanging on for dear life to the bars on the outside of the car windows, keeping a weather eye alert for cops.

As I remarked earlier, St. Pius was not altogether happy with my presence within its walls. The unhappiness was mutual, except during the fifth grade. Sister Elsa Marie, my fifth grade teacher, singled me out as the boy to stay after school to dust erasers and wash the blackboard. Neither of us regarded this as punishment, although I was generally regarded as the Peck's Bad Boy of the South Side. Sister Elsa Marie was evidently something of a psychologist, for she realized that I was going through a crisis. She would talk with me about my problems at home.

The country was deep in the depression, and father's business had dwindled to a point where he could not face the dismal reality. Like Amanda's husband in Tennessee Williams's *The Glass Menagerie,* he had "fallen in love with long distance." We didn't see much of him at home anymore.

My mother, though, was stouthearted enough for two. When the burden of feeding the children and keeping up our spirits fell upon her frail shoulders, she started a lively business at home, and we all pitched in to help. Neighbors and people from all over the quarter were knocking on our front door to order her angel food cakes and superlative homemade mayonnaise. The boys made deliveries, and our sisters helped with the baking, but Mom herself dripped the olive oil into the fresh egg yolks for the finest mayonnaise west of Cincinnati.

In addition to providing for her family, my mother also found the time to help others. She worked with the nuns of the Convent of the Good Shepherd in their home for girls in trouble. She founded the Mothers' Club at St. Louis University High and gave time to the Blind Girls' Home. Later, as the family grew up, she took a job with the Missouri Commission for the Blind.

After my unexpected graduation from grade school, Mother, using all her connections and ingenuity, managed to get me admitted to the prestigious St. Louis University High School in the fall of 1934. She hoped that I could benefit not only from the high academic standards and tough classical curriculum, but from the strict discipline of the Jesuit fathers in charge.

Three days after I was enrolled I was out again. The Jesuits did not approve of my business activities.

I had already shown a talent for business while I was in grade school. I had set up a miniature golf course in our backyard. After making the full circuit, the player would hole out through the wall of our garage. If he wanted to go around again, he had to cough up another nickel for a fresh ball.

But my high school enterprise that brought about my downfall consisted in selling used textbooks to pay for my own books. The only trouble was that some of my stock-in-trade included eighth-grade texts that I was selling to ninth-grade students. Father Bowdern, the principal, did not approve of the practice, and despite my plea of *caveat emptor,* I was suspended.

My mother's intervention got me readmitted on a promise of good behavior. My exemplary behavior lasted through the winter, but spring brought disaster. I had a fistfight with a classmate that resulted in my wrecking a mouthful of his expensive prosthetic dental work. My mother reimbursed his parents for the repairs, but Father Bowdern had had enough of the youngest Cervantes. This time I was out for good.

Those days I remember with great pain and embarrassment, especially when I emphasize to my own children the importance of a good education, always pointing to the difficulties confronting a high school dropout. It is true that hard work and persistence will overcome many handicaps, but I still regret not going on with my formal education. My failure at St. Louis University High was the only real opportunity in my life that I missed. Despite early struggles, my career has been far from unsuccessful, but I'm sure that continuing my education would have made my life richer and deeper and given me a greater appreciation of all the good things that have come my way over the years.

I also regret the profound disappointment I caused my mother, who had made sacrifices to give me the best schooling available. I must say she never held my boyhood foibles against me, and I hope I made up for her trust in later years when, crippled by arthritis, she was helped to a seat in the impressive rotunda of the St. Louis City Hall with its monumental staircase, its glittering chandeliers and colorful flags, where she could watch the television cameras focused on her wayward youngest son as he took the oath of office as mayor of the city.

In those dark days of May, 1935, when my smart-alecky world suddenly fell apart, I knew instinctively that I would have to make a fresh start. Overnight I decided to leave home. I have made thousands of snap decisions since, a few of which I have regretted, but not this first one. When I told my mother that I was going west, I was surprised that she raised no objections. Later I learned that she had anticipated some such move on my part, and had sought professional advice.

"Let him go," said Dr. X. "Let him find his own level. He has to work out his problems his own way."

So a few months before my fifteenth birthday, with a quarter and a few dimes in my pocket, I started hitchhiking for California, where, people said, the sun was always shining and everybody was getting rich.

II

Thumbing my way through the Dust Bowl offered few hardships. Motorists were usually friendly to a neatly dressed teen-age hitchhiker, and aside from suspicious farm wives in rural Arkansas, enough housewives who responded to my knock on the back door were ready to trade a meal for cutting the grass or some other odd job. I learned other tricks, too. A firehouse usually offered a place to sleep, and sometimes a meal as well. Firemen seemed always ready to interrupt a card game for a few words with a young wayfarer. And if all else failed I could always try the parish house next to the church.

When I hit Dallas, Texans were celebrating the centennial of their Lone Star Republic with a Texas-size fair. St. Louisans were still talking about their own world's fair—the Louisiana Purchase Expositions of 1904—but I had never seen anything as gigantic or exciting as the Dallas show. I thought I'd stick around for a while, so I got a job as busboy in the Maxwell House Coffee pavilion. Later I worked as a "coolie," pulling a rickshaw for footsore visitors. It was harder work but the tips were bigger.

I spent my Dallas lunch hours at the Bell Telephone Company's exhibit, playing their lottery. The winners got a free long-distance call to any place in the country. I was pretty lucky and got to call St. Louis almost every day to talk to my family and best pals. Those phone calls, combined with the fading summer, brought on a wave of homesickness, and I decided to put off seeing California. When the leaves began to turn and the evening breezes grew sharp with the nip of autumn I was back on Juniata Street.

Inevitably my schooling was resumed by maternal request. This time, however, my mother gave up on the idea of a classical education. Every morning I boarded the Grand Street trolley to Bell Avenue for classes at Hadley Vocational High School.

My heart wasn't in it, though. I had had my first taste of freedom and I liked it. I had proved to myself that I could make it on my own. The big, hard, cruel world had its soft spots, and I wanted to probe them further. When the first chill of winter swept St. Louis, I began to think of that famous California sunshine again. Soon afterward I was once more headed west.

Hitchhiking went smoothly until I hit the vast, open spaces of Texas, where cars were as few and far between as gas stations. When I tired of sticking out my thumb without getting a ride, I hopped my first freight.

I had plenty of company. Times were still tight and the exodus from the Dust Bowl was still on. There were ten or fifteen men huddled inside every boxcar I got into. I wasn't always lucky enough to make the inside, though, and I learned to ride the suspension rods underneath the cars—a dirty, precarious business. You not only risked slipping off through dust and cinders to the murderous flanged wheels, but you had to survive smoke suffocation in long tunnels in the Rockies. I remember a train stopping outside the Moffat tunnel in Colorado while a platoon of railroad "bulls" (guards) charged alongside the cars to brush off the free-riders who didn't realize it was for their own welfare.

During my freight-hopping days I developed a genuine affection for the daily newspapers, although in recent years many a journalist has doubted I ever had such sentiments. When I was sneaking rides over the Rockies in unheated boxcars, I used to wrap myself in newspapers to keep warm.

Some nights I spent in hobo camps. The food was not quite up to some I have sampled at the Jockey Club in Madrid or at Joe Kemoll's in St. Louis, but when a boy is hungry the most primitive tin-can mulligan, seasoned with no-questions-asked fellowship, is as satisfying as a pressed duck at the Tour d'Argent in Paris.

I finally reached my Eldorado—San Francisco. A magic name and a fascinating city, but the streets were not paved with gold. I did manage to keep body and soul together by washing dishes in exchange for restaurant meals and by sleeping in the Ferry Building at the foot of Market Street until I was chased out by a night watchman.

Meanwhile I was trying to ship out as deck hand on one of the aristocratic-looking liners I had seen gliding out through the Golden Gate bound for the Orient. I haunted the Embarcadero for weeks trying for a berth, but the ship's officers wouldn't hire me because I was not a union seaman and the unions refused to give me a membership card because I had no seagoing experience.

One day, while I was making these futile trips from dock to dock, my low spirits probably showing, a late-model car pulled up even with me at the curb. The driver hailed me and invited me to lunch. I was ravenous as well as curious. I accepted.

My unexpected host's name was Griff, and he had been a subway trainman in New York. He was a heavy-set man who looked pretty old to a teen-ager—he must have been at least forty-five or fifty—and he had a well-filled wallet. He was lonesome, he said, and was anxious for a little company. As I got to know him better I discovered the reason for his loneliness: He could be pretty obnoxious at times. But before we parted company I had seen Yosemite, Sequoia National Park, and a lot of the California coast from the window of Griff's car.

By this time I had decided that the real California did not measure up to the myths. Anyhow I was tired of spinning my wheels in San Francisco. I hit the eastbound road again by thumb and by freight, heading for St. Louis and home.

I was not heading back to school again; of that I was quite sure. I tried juggling boxes as stock clerk at International Shoe Company at Thirteenth and Washington; that proved too tame. Jerking sodas behind the counter at Keller's drug store at Brannon and Chippewa was a little more exciting. At least I was held up there at the point of a gun for the only time in my life. I was feeling very brave and wanted to argue with the robber until he hit me on the head and Mr. Keller said, "Give him the money, Fonsie." I threw a handful of change at him but he reached into the cash register and helped himself to the bills. I didn't see much future in that job either.

So when my friend Joe Scannell told me he was driving to Los Angeles to get married and asked me to go along and share expenses, I jumped at the chance. My sister Victoria came along too. It cost each of us sixteen dollars.

Joe's girl friend's brother, Bud Hoppe, gave me a job a few days after we got to the coast, and I became an apprentice paperhanger at a dollar a day. It wasn't exactly paper that I hung, but "Sanitas," a heavy, canvas wall covering then very much in vogue in Southern California. In no time I had worked up to five dollars a day and moved from South Los Angeles to Hollywood.

I was sharing an apartment with Joe Harris, whose brother-in-law lived near me in St. Louis, and John Kennedy, a cartoonist from Minneapolis. Joe had come to Hollywood with a magazine crew and was later chauffeur for actor Joseph Schildkraut. Kennedy was drawing for Schlessinger's *Looney Toons* and *Merrie Melodies*. He was the proud owner of a magnificent, bright-yellow Dusenberg, whose previous owner had made it three feet longer by adding a false radiator.

We were living on the fringes of the movie crowd. William S. Hart lived next door (I don't know where his horse lived). We often rubbed elbows with Mickey Rooney, and we were invited to a swimming party at Ramon Navarro's pool. Navarro was known as the great lover of the silent films, but had apparently developed a gay, new life-style since films began to talk. At any rate we escaped the party early.

I felt I had better get a job more fitting to my new social station. When people asked me what line of work I was in, I was a little embarrassed to tell them I was a paperhanger. The profession was getting a bad name anyway, since a former paperhanger named Adolf Hitler was being mentioned in the papers pretty often. I began to moonlight as a salesman in a National Shirt Shop. It was cleaner work than hanging Sanitas and paid more, so I made it my full-time occupation while I started to look around for the big chance.

I began attending night classes at Hollywood High School, although I am not sure that my good attendance record was due to a delayed appreciation of education or to the presence of Lana Turner in one of the courses.

It was about this time that I discovered my forte.

I was not yet out of my teens, but I found that I had a talent that was to serve me and my city well when I became mayor twenty-five years later.

It would seem that I was a born promoter.

III

During the period I was shuttling between the halls of learning and the open road, Bernard F. Dickmann had been swept into St. Louis City Hall on the crest of the Democratic tidal wave generated by the election of Franklin D. Roosevelt.

The St. Louis City Hall has an aura of faded Gallic magnificence about it. Its facade is modeled after the sixteenth-century Hôtel de Ville in Paris, in honor of the city's French origins. It has an impressive entrance hall, crystal chandeliers, huge rooms with twenty-foot ceilings, and symbolic murals representing the Louisiana Purchase, the centenary celebration of which coincided with the dedication of the building. However, when Mayor Dickmann moved in he was disagreeably surprised to find that despite its grandiose dimensions, the mayor's office and adjoining reception hall were rundown and seedy. fore spent some $3000 of the city's money to build himself a bathroom with toilet and shower.

When Dickmann ran for reelection the unfriendly press made a great to-do about his wasting taxpayers' money for his own comfort. His opponent mounted bathtubs on flatbed trucks to parade the streets with such signs as "Is this the way you want your taxes spent?" Apparently it was not, for Bernard Dickmann (who became a close friend of mind in later years) was defeated.

As a consequence, no mayor for the next twenty-seven years dared to spend one cent for maintaining a decent office. When I moved in, the mayor's office and adjoining reception hall were run-down and seedy. The old green carpet was threadbare and torn, the ancient leather chairs were scuffed and worn, the sofas sagged, and the whole drab, dingy set-up was not worthy of a whistle-stop constable's office.

When I decided to ask the board of aldermen for $50,000 to brighten up Room 200, my staff was horrified. "Mayor, don't do it," they said. "They'll run you out of town." But I went ahead and did it anyway.

I called in William Bernoudy, one of the city's top interior decorators, and told him, "Bill, I want you to design an office the city will be proud of." Then we threw out the old rugs and broken-down furniture and tattered drapes. We sent to Puerto Rico for a few hundred square yards of red carpeting with the city seal woven into it. The City Art Museum sent over experts to brighten up the murals. The crystal chandeliers had their sparkle restored. We got rid of the old wooden fence where the uniformed cop used to stand guard and the reporters in shirt sleeves would litter the landscape with crumpled copy paper. We installed rich-looking, velvety sofas for people waiting for appointments.

When it was all finished we called in the press for a preview. Then we invited city employees and prominent citizens in delegations of two thousand every Sunday for open house on six successive Sundays to see what we had done to the shabby old premises. The press waxed enthusiastic, and the Sunday editions produced layouts in color.

So one mayor spends $3,000 of the taxpayers' money and loses an election, while another spends $50,000 and wins rave notices. The new office became a political asset as well as a thing of beauty.

I tell this story here because it was in Hollywood that I learned the fundamentals of public relations.

During the late thirties the rhumba craze had struck Hollywood. At Monty Prosser's La Conga, on Vine just below Hollywood Boulevard, a fellow who called himself Carlos Fernandez (I think his real name was something like Manny Steinberg) gave rhumba lessons during the cocktail hour. He also gave me a fertile idea.

Clara Bow, the "It Girl," owned a nightclub called "The It Cafe" in the Plaza Hotel. I went to Jack Clark, the Plaza manager, with a proposition: I would organize a series of rhumba contests on eight Tuesday nights (Tuesday was the leanest night of the week) with a grand finale of the weekly winners on the ninth Tuesday. The Cervantes Rhumba Club (as yet existing only in my mind) would furnish the contestants. All I wanted was 25 percent of the take on contest nights. Jack offered 10 percent and we settled for 15.

The Tuesday nights were so successful that I soon organized an agency to expand the operation. In a few months I was running rhumba contests at such Hollywood nightspots as La Conga, Ciro's, La Bomba, and biggest, brassiest of them all, El Rancho Grande on La Cienega Boulevard. El Rancho was under the direction of Wallace Beery's brother Noah, and its decor resembled the set for an old Western movie (it probably was).

The Cervantes contests overflowed into weekends and matinees, usually jam-packed. The town was plastered with Cervantes Rhumba Club posters. A column, "Rhumba Round the Town," ghost-written by Joe Harris, appeared under my by-line in a weekly paper. I had so many contests going that the national dance-offs had to be held in the American Legion Stadium. A lot of characters who later became celebrities—major and minor—came to shake their gluteal muscles in competition. Lena Horne appeared several times, well chaperoned by her mother, to begin her career at La Conga.

As master of ceremonies I had the time of my life extending my hands over the winning couple while the band played crescendo chords and I prepared to present the loving cup. My incarnation as MC for rhumba contests in Hollywood was also an excellent apprenticeship for a political career. I was vaccinated against stagefright. I learned to be at ease when facing a crowd, to think on my feet, and to talk off the top of my head.

Shortly after his twenty-first birthday, A. J. Cervantes was sitting on top of the world. He had plenty of folding money in his wallet, good clothes on his back (I was always a fussy dresser), and a brand-new convertible paid for in cash.

I was driving my new car down Highland Avenue one Sunday morning in December, 1941, when my Hollywood adventure came to an abrupt end. My car radio reported that Japanese planes were attacking Pearl Harbor. Would California be invaded next?

Next morning I was standing in line to enlist in the merchant marine. I had always been intrigued by those recruiting posters inviting young men to see the world through a porthole, and I saw a chance to make up for my frustration in San Francisco and still serve the country at war. A few days later I was on a train—sitting in the inside this time, courtesy of the U.S. government—heading east to become a seafaring man.

IV

I still shiver when I remember boarding the cutter in Boston harbor bound for Gallup's Island, wearing my light, snappy California coat in the dead of a New England winter.

I spent most of a year on the island training to be a radio officer. That was on weekdays. On weekends I'd go into Boston to keep my hand in as a promoter. With a few fellow cadets I'd rent a ballroom, borrow girls from the USO, and fill the room at a dollar a head for dancing and all the beer a man could drink. This went on for nine months, and it was with a twinge of regret that I received my commission and travel orders for the West Coast, even though winter would be coming around again.

While waiting for a ship in San Francisco, sitting in the Sir Francis Drake and signing checks at government expense, I began to wonder if the months spent learning about kilocycles and frequency modulation had dulled my talent for salesmanship. The holiday season was approaching, so I managed to pick up a little extra money selling Christmas shirts and ties at a chain haberdashery.

Finally the call came, and we left to join our ship in Seattle. It was a cargo ship carrying I-forget-what to the Aleutian Islands. We weighed anchor for Dutch Harbor in the wake of a blizzard.

Being "Sparks" on a freighter, sitting for hours with a headset clamped to my ears, pounding the brass now and then to forward a routine message, was not the most exciting way to fight a war. The merchant marine did make good on the promise of the recruiting poster. I did see the world—from the Arctic Circle to the Indian Ocean and from the South Pacific to the Mediterranean—but except for one hairy incident, mine was a pretty dull war. And my quota of excitement was unauthorized.

While we were lying in Dutch Harbor with nothing much for "Sparks" to do, things were popping elsewhere in the Aleutians. We had retaken Kiska from the Japanese, but Attu was still holding out, and our planes were trying to soften it up from the air before our amphibious attack. Loafing around the air base, I talked a couple of airmen into taking me along on the next few bombing runs. I made myself useful. I sat next to the bomb bay and if a bomb got stuck I could stretch out a leg and kick it loose.

The Japanese anti-aircraft gunners on Attu were not too accurate, but one day they got lucky. We were not blown out of the sky, but we were hit badly enough so we had to make a forced landing on Amchitka. The crippled plane stood on its nose after we made the runway, and we were all cut and bruised. Fortunately, Amchitka was conveniently close to Attu, but it was still several hundred miles away from my ship at Dutch Harbor. The Army Air Force colonel couldn't understand what the merchant marine officer was doing on a combat mission, and his vocal blistering raised welts on my otherwise calloused ego. Thereafter, I stayed close to the radio shack, whether the ship was in Ceylon or Tasmania.

Except in Murmansk.

The German U-boats were raising murderous hell with our convoys on the Murmansk run, and the Russian government was offering a bonus to merchant seamen volunteering to sail with a ship carrying supplies to the Soviet Union. I volunteered.

There was a certain tension after our convoy left Hampton Roads, for the casualty list of American sailors lost to submarines on the Murmansk run was depressing. However, we crossed the Atlantic and the North Sea and rounded North Cape without seeing a periscope. The most exciting sight on that voyage was the sun shining at midnight. The second most exciting was that of the Russians coming aboard at Murmansk with their big, black bags to distribute the promised bonuses.

I went ashore with a pocketful of rubles intending to paint the town red, white, and blue. It wasn't easy. First there was the language gap; nobody understood what we wanted. Second, Murmansk was the first port I'd ever seen where nobody was lying in wait to guide the way to someplace devoted to separating a sailor from his money. Third, there apparently was no such place.

When I finally located a joint supposed to cater to the fun-loving serviceman, it looked to me more like an old folks' home. The five or six oldsters sitting around stared at me when I came in, but they didn't object when I pulled out my wad of rubles and bought a round of drinks for the house. I suppose the gesture cost me about sixty-five cents because I got back a handful of kopeks in change. I raised my glass of vodka in a toast of international good will.

I drank, and decided at once that the potentiality of vodka as an instrument of good feeling was strictly limited. It may have been because the comrades were making vodka from potatoes in wartime, as someone told me, but whatever it was shook me to the soles of my feet. The cocktails our air force boys concocted out of de-icing fluid was sheer nectar compared to Murmansk vodka.

However, if this was the wine of the country I could be as game as the next man, despite the threat to my digestive system. I bought another round for the assembled gaffers, apparently all veterans of the

Napoleonic campaign of 1812. Then I took off in further search of the gay night life. If there was any, I never found it.

I did find a curio shop where I picked up two little hand-carved bears and a few phonograph records. Then I went out into the midnight sunshine and made my way back to the ship.

My shipmates had fared no better. We spent the rest of our stay in port on board playing chess.

When all our cargo had been unloaded and we were ready to start back through U-boat Lane, the Russians produced their crowning surprise. The comrade commissar came aboard to collect all our unspent rubles. Wartime exchange regulations, we were told, forbade the export of Soviet currency.

Looking back on my visit to Murmansk from the perspective of City Hall, I can almost understand how a city department head feels when he finds an end-of-year surplus in his budget allotment and rushes to try and spend it instead of turning it back. A good mayor, on the other hand, must try to recapture every unspent nickel. But Radio Officer Cervantes, on the homeward leg of his voyage around North Cape, bitterly resented the fact that his "hero's bonus" had netted him just two carved bears, some phonograph recordings he could not understand, and two of the most ghastly drinks that ever have insulted his stomach.

III

Cuspidors and Flowers

The Amateur and the Brawling Aldermen

My first step on the road to Room 200 of St. Louis City Hall was the chance remark by a cab driver who drove for a taxi firm of which I was half-owner. I got into the taxicab business quite by accident: The original sole owner gave me a half-interest in lieu of unpaid insurance premiums.

Insurance was my business when I came home from the war. The country had an oversupply of radio operators and the rhumba business didn't seem to have much of a future, at least in St. Louis. I came back to my home town determined to settle down and make a serious living, and I guess I picked insurance for three reasons: I would be following in the footsteps of my father who was good at it; I felt I was a born salesman; and I could sell insurance without making a capital investment for stock in trade.

My office was a room in my mother's flat. With the family gone from the nest, she had given up the big house which was my birthplace. She still lived on Juniata Street, though. She couldn't separate herself from the old South Side neighborhood. One room was big enough to accommodate my business: My first month's take was something like fifty-five dollars.

But I was losing no time in putting my Hollywood talents to work. I tramped the streets with the pockets of my uniform bulging with my business cards. I did a pretty thorough job of covering the town from Kingshighway to the riverfront.

One night, just as I was getting home for dinner, the phone rang. It was Elmer Nonnenkamp, who had taken one of my cards (with a noncommittal nod) at the Manchester Bank a few weeks earlier.

"Are you the fella in uniform who came in the bank the other day and said he handled truck insurance?"

I was indeed.

"Look," he said, "I need an insurance man right now to close a deal. How soon can you get down to Zoeder's garage at Seventh and Franklin?"

"Right away," I told him.

I found the banker in Zoeder's grimy little office. Manchester Bank was financing the sale of Zoeder's fleet of trucks to his drivers on the installment plan.

"This here's Joe Doakes," Zoeder would say. "He's buying the '41 International Tractor."

Nonnenkamp would ask me what the insurance would cost on the tractor mentioned, and I'd quote the premium figure.

The banker would write one check for the price of the truck and another for the insurance, and Doakes would drive his truck home. The process was repeated some twenty times before I went home myself.

It was ten o'clock before I ran up the steps of the flat on Juniata Street. My pockets were full of checks. My commission on the evening's premiums must have come close to two thousand dollars. I could not resist the temptation of emptying my pockets on the living room table where my mother was sitting.

My mother stood up suddenly and looked around apprehensively as though expecting the police to rush up the stairs right behind me.

"Where did you get all this money?" she demanded. It just wasn't possible that anyone could earn that much money honestly in the few hours since dinner time.

It was my good luck, of course, that Emmett Concannon, Manchester Bank's regular insurance man, was not available when the Zoeder deal came to a head. Emmett finally forgave me and we became good friends.

I frequently went around to Seventh and Franklin to take care of

Zoeder's drivers, and I noted that there was almost always a fat man sitting on a barrel outside the garage. One day late in 1946 the fat man hailed me. "Hey, do you sell taxicab insurance?"

"Sure," I answered. I hadn't up to then, but there was no reason why I shouldn't.

"We're getting some hack permits from City Hall pretty soon," he said. "I'll flag you when we do."

I didn't put much stock in the fat man's announcement, because taxicab licenses were not easy to come by. I learned later that the fat man on the barrel knew his way around City Hall. He knew Bombie Spicuzzi, who was the Republican committeeman of the Sixth Ward. Sure enough, he wangled the license and it wasn't long before I was writing a policy on a '39 LaSalle, the first of what was to become a fleet of taxis.

Insuring cabs wasn't very profitable at first. My commission on the first taxi policy, as I recall, was 5 percent of a monthly premium of eighteen dollars—about ninety cents. Even with the fleet growing to ten or twelve cabs it was not exactly a gold mine. Trucks were more rewarding. I worked with Ed Nalley, a Freuhauf truck salesman, arranging GI loans for veterans who wanted to go into trucking. Insuring the heavy jobs brought a commission of 25 percent.

However, that old LaSalle grew into the Laclede Cab Company, with thirty to forty cabs and an attractive insurance account. Charlie Seal, who ran the show, offered me office space if I would help with the operation. Charlie was a fine mechanic and loved to tinker with engines, but he was bored stiff with management details. So I moved my office from home. The arrangement was working out all right, except for one little detail: The insurance premiums were not being paid.

Finally Charlie Seal offered me half-interest in Laclede if I would write off what he owed me for back insurance premiums. I hesitated a long time before giving him an answer, because there was an aroma hovering over some aspects of the taxi business that was a long way from the odor of sanctity. For instance, there was the matter of "Liner loads."

"Liner loads" owed their name to Willie Liner, an old-time St. Louis cab driver who had a lucrative sideline. The French have an elegant word for characters with his avocation—*proxénète*—but the English language has a shorter and uglier word of four letters. At any rate, Liner had a long roster of names and addresses of ladies who were ready and willing to accommodate lonely strangers in search of fun and games, and too many cabbies who came after him were just as eager for the same kind of money.

I disliked finding myself in a position similar to that of a certain French archbishop in the early part of the century. His Grace had been flooded with complaints about the infamous brothel doing a land-office business right around the corner from the cathedral. The faithful loathed running into off-duty ladies of the evening while on their way to or from Mass. The archdiocese thereupon arranged to purchase the building in which the bordello was located, intending to convert it into an orphanage or other worthier purpose. However, the year was 1914, and just as His Grace completed the transaction, but before he could evict the tenants, the First World War broke out and a national moratorium froze all leases. So the archbishop found himself titular landlord of the biggest bawdy house in town.

Although not relishing the role of titular operator of Liner-load cabs, I accepted the half-interest in Laclede on condition that I would have complete authority to clean up the fleet. I started by firing drivers who doubled as pimps. I then got rid of those with a police record and refused to hire anyone who had one. We put uniforms on the drivers and started an inspection program that guaranteed clean cabs. I wanted a new image for the company so that old ladies wouldn't hesitate to call a Laclede Cab after dark.

I went deeply into debt to install two-way radios in each of our cabs—the first electronic dispatch system in town. We offered patrons a free ride if our cab didn't pick them up within ten minutes of their phone call. In five years the number of calls rose from 800 a month to 80,000.

When Orville Ludwig took over the day-to-day operation, I could begin to think about setting up a separate office for my insurance enterprise, which was growing.

II

In the fall of 1948 I was swapping yarns with one of our Laclede drivers who had become a supervisor, when he suddenly said, "You know, Al, you ought to run for alderman."

"Ed, you're kidding," I replied, but I knew he wasn't. Ed Sullivan was one of those Irishmen from North St. Louis who are born with politics in their blood. "Why?"

"I dunno," he said. "Just a hunch you'd be good at it."

I had met only one alderman in my life, and I didn't much admire the sample. He had approached me when there was a matter of taxicab regulation before the board and he had let me know that a certain amount of well-placed wampum might persuade a decisive number of braves to desist from scalping the cab industry.

Still, Ed Sullivan's remark intrigued me. I asked around and found that the legislative body of the city of St. Louis consisted of one alderman elected from each of twenty-eight districts (wards) and a president of the board elected citywide. I investigated further and found that I lived in the Fifteenth Ward.

By this time I had taken what is undoubtedly the most important decision in my life. Having fallen in love with a perfectly stunning girl named Carmen (she bore no more relation to Bizet's heroine than I did to Don Quixote's creator; neither of us speak Spanish), I had persuaded her to marry me. When the political bug bit me were were living with our first child, Judy, in a four-family flat on Botanical Avenue across Tower Grove Park from Juniata Street. Carmen thought maybe it would be a good idea to run for alderman.

As the rankest of amateurs I didn't know the first thing about how to throw my hat into the ring. So I went back to Ed Sullivan, who for years had been ringing doorbells for the Democrats in the Second Ward.

"See your committeeman," Sullivan said. I'm sure he thought I was putting him on when I asked him what a committeeman was, but he patiently explained that the title belonged to the number one boy in a party's ward organization.

The only organization in the Fifteenth Ward I knew of was the 39th Street Businessmen's Association. Had I consulted them they would undoubtedly have sent me to the Republican committeeman, for the ward was heavily Republican. However, Ed Sullivan was my political adviser, and he sent me to Democrat Jerry Cleary.

It was a cold January day when I first phoned Mr. Cleary.

"He's with the president," said a voice on the phone. "Mr. Cleary's in Washington with President Truman."

I was properly impressed. I promptly joined the ward Democratic organization. I didn't learn until later that Mr. Cleary was in Washington as one member of a large Missouri delegation attending the inauguration of fellow-Missouri Democrat, Harry Truman.

Meanwhile I had met Jack Murphy, a bright and affable young man working in the office of Morris Shenker, who, as we will learn later, was fated to play an important role in my life. When I retained Murphy as my attorney, I mentioned casually that I was thinking of running for alderman. Murphy said he thought he could give me a little help; he was always given to understatement.

"You ought to see my Uncle George," said Murphy.

Jack Murphy's Uncle George was officially Jury Commissioner of the city. Unofficially he was one of the big guns of the Democratic party, with a range that carried beyond the borders of Missouri, and as long as there was a Missourian in the White House, as far as Washington. I went to see him, hat in hand.

George Murphy was a short, stocky man who even looked like a .politician. He reminded me in many ways of Chicago Mayor Richard Daley. Someone once described him as "a fireplug with a hat on." Politics were as important to Uncle George as his family. In fact there was no hard-and-fast dividing line between the two. Any relative of his who wanted a political job had it.

When I told George Murphy I wanted to be an alderman he said: "It takes work to be a good alderman, and it takes money to finance a campaign. Still want to run?" I said I did.

Inasmuch as Fifteenth Ward Committeeman Cleary owed his job to Uncle George, a Murphy nod was tantamount to an official blessing. By the end of January, 1949, the regular Democratic organization of the Fifteenth Ward had a candidate for alderman in the spring elections—an ambitious young businessman named Cervantes.

Had I any political sense I would have been scared to death. The good burghers of the South Side traditionally voted Republican, usually for someone with a German name, just as the Irish of the North Side traditionally voted Democratic. In 1949, Mayor Kaufmann, Comptroller Nolte, and a majority of the board of aldermen were Republicans. True, the Missouri Democrats had mustered a fine majority the year before to keep Truman in the White House, but nobody expected the Democratic tide to flood the Fifteenth Ward in 1949.

First of all, there was a rift in the party. A group that wanted to control ward patronage had put up Ike Laubenthal, a war veteran with American Legion backing and a good German name. When I had cleared that hurdle by winning in the primaries, I had a much higher jump ahead. The incumbent was Republican Louis A. Lange, a veteran of four terms and another possessor of a good German name. What chance did a guy with a name like Alfonso Cervantes stand?

I wasn't intimidated. When addressing gatherings dominated by the good burghers and their hausfraus, I spoke of my fine German grandmother Kussenberger and my admirable mother Victoria Kussenberger (the women of the Fifteenth Ward knew that was not political hyperbole). As for the Irish Democrats who had somehow wandered into the ward's electoral register, the names of Cleary and Murphy were like the stamp of sterling on silver.

The opening night of my campaign, when I addressed the ward workers at Colombo's Tavern on Kingshighway and Shaw, was notable for me, because the Democratic candidate for mayor, Joe Darst, came by and shook my hand. But drinking beer with the hardworking precinct captains afterward, I sized up the ethnic makeup of my supporters and their ladies who were sitting at a table with Carmen. George Werner and Nellie Fuerst seemed to be about the only Teutonic representatives, while Jim Fitzsimmons was flanked by Mary Margaret "Sis" Bresnahan, Mary Ball, Irene Burke, and Catherine Sheeran. It looked like it was going to be a long, hard pull.

I know it is common practice for politicians to declare that they owe everything to their wives. I suspect it is often true. I know that I could not have survived the ordeal of my first campaign without Carmen. Her loyalty, her intelligent advice, and her sheer persistence were just what an apprentice needed. While we pounded frost-bitten feet on cold pavements during the bitter months of February and early March, she proved a far better campaigner than the candidate. We worked opposite sides of the street ringing doorbells, and though pregnant with our second child, A.J., Jr., she outrang me by at least ten to one. Where I would accept an invitation to step into a warm living room and give my spiel about how I was in favor of lower taxes and higher property values, better police protection and garbage collection, more efficient street cleaning and trimming the trees that lined the streets, Carmen would have rung the doorbell, handed out my literature, asked the householder to vote for her husband, and moved on to the next doorbell. By the time I had reached the next corner she had been shivering and stamping her feet to keep warm while I was still glowing with the warmth of half a dozen living rooms. She was not always pleased with my modus operandi, but she went on ringing doorbells.

We had the opposition worried. Our spies brought word that the other camp was planning to distribute tracts claiming that a vote for Cervantes would be wasted, because I had not lived in the ward long enough to be eligible to serve. Hell, I had been born in the ward, and I wasn't going to be put off by campaign charges that could not be effectively answered in the time left before election.

During the last days I was out early, driving around with my brother-in-law, Irv Karches, and my good friends Bill Stephens and Bill Boody, trying to smell out the opposition's skullduggery. On the fourth day we picked up the scent.

At the intersection of Grand Avenue and DeTonty we intercepted two old men with canvas bags slung over their shoulders climbing the high terraces to decorate every doorstep with anti-Cervantes propaganda. Bill jumped out of the car and grabbed one of their pink sheets. The black headline read: "DON'T WASTE YOUR VOTE!," as predicted.

"Boy, am I glad I caught you guys in time. These bills are supposed to be delivered over on Gravois," said Bill.

"But the boss told us," one of the old men began, "that we. . . ."

"I know he did. But it was a mistake. A good thing I got to you in time." And Bill helped the old boys into the back of my car so we could drive them over to Gravois and out of our ward. There was no reason they should have recognized me.

We intercepted another pair on Arsenal Street, and Bill convinced them they should hand out their pink fliers on Utah Street where I wasn't running.

My opponent naturally was furious when he found out what had happened to his handbills, particularly when he had to pay for their delivery to the wrong voters.

My election was a close squeak, but I won, and when the votes were counted we held a victory celebration in our little apartment on

Botanical Avenue—Jim, George, Sis, Mary, Irene, Nellie, and Catherine. Even Uncle George stopped by to shake my hand and congratulate Carmen.

III

Getting elected had been a fight—figuratively speaking.

Getting seated in the solemn chambers of the board of aldermen was another fight—literally speaking.

By unseating the venerable Louis Lange by the razor-thin margin of 48 votes out of 7,856 cast, I had upset the comfortable Republican majority which had controlled the board for years. The new Democratic majority of fifteen to fourteen carried with it the power to organize the board, control the committees and appoint staff. The Republicans were not going to take their loss lying down, particularly as they had also lost the mayor's office, the comptroller's office, and control of the patronage offices on the first floor of City Hall—collector of revenue, recorder of deeds, and license collector.

I had no idea that the Republican hostility was going to zero in on me, for I didn't quite realize that my one vote could swing the balance. Besides, a friendly atmosphere seemed to prevail that April day in 1949 when I entered the chamber to be sworn in.

For me it was an impressive moment. The great room was heavy with history. High on the walls were murals depicting the varied life of the city. Around the inside of the cupola were portraits of distinguished city fathers like LeBaume and Mullanphy staring down sternly at the transitory proceedings on the floor. The clusters of big, white light globes in the chandeliers were like planets in an orrery going around their private sun.

I made my way through the crowd of well-wishers that packed the chamber wall to wall, heading toward the desk bearing the shiny new nameplate that read:

A. J. CERVANTES   15th WARD

Beside the desk on the floor was a brand-new cuspidor, which I learned was also a perquisite of office. In the retinue that escorted me were Carmen, carrying our soon-to-be-born second child, our daughter Judy,

Carmen's mother, and her sister Jerry. Proud with her corsage was my mother, who knew City Hall better than I did from having worked with former Mayor Barney Dickmann. My three sisters, Kay, Tory, and Ginny, were with her. Closing the family ranks was my brother Lu, who had just been ordained a Jesuit priest.

The semicircle of desk tops in that huge room was one mass of congratulatory flowers. The floral pieces were too numerous for the newly elected aldermen from the odd-numbered wards, and they overflowed onto the empty desks of the incumbents from the even-numbered wards who had not been up for election.

The president of the board, Charles Albanese, was the only Republican holding a major office to escape the Democratic sweep, as his job was not up for election in 1949. He made the most of his remnant of power. As soon as the invocation was over, he recognized Republican Alderman J. Ray Weinbrenner, who rose to make a point of order. Weinbrenner started reading a diatribe which challenged the right of some of the newly elected aldermen to serve.

Suddenly I realized that I was the one under attack. I closed my eyes and seemed to see those pink handbills with the black type: "DON'T WASTE YOUR VOTE ... Cervantes is not eligible to represent your ward. . . . He has not fulfilled the residency requirements!"

The new aldermen were filing up to the rostrum to be sworn in. The clerk reading the roll had passed the Cs! He was a Republican, of course; the newly elected board had not yet been organized.

The chamber began to buzz.

The clerk had nearly finished the swearing in. He had also skipped the name of Ray Egan, Democrat from the Seventeenth Ward.

The buzzing had become a roar. A power play was in the making. The Republicans were taking advantage of their final moments of holding the staff jobs. By deliberately omitting the names of Cervantes and Egan from the swearing-in roll call, the clerk had restored the Republican majority for the moment.

"Point of order, Mr. President. . . ." A Democrat had risen to question the omissions.

Patriarchal Mr. Luecke, Republican parliamentarian, ruled that the clerk should continue with the list as read.

Whereupon all hell broke loose.

Television, that infant medium, suddenly had an unscheduled spectacular, a noonday rival for the Friday-night fights. The action was livelier and the language was something never heard in prime time. And the Marquess of Queensbury rules were not observed.

The argument shifted from words to action when Democratic Sheriff Tom Callanan rushed the clerk's desk and took a solid swing at parliamentarian Luecke.

When the live audience got over the shock of the assault on the dignified septuagenarian, the combat zone expanded immediately. Everybody seemed to be fighting to get into the fight. The TV cameras brought the incredible melee into every bar and living room tuned in on KSD-TV. Fists and flowers flew as the zoom lenses focused now on the president's dais, now on an individual slugging match. Screaming profanity reached astonished viewers with no network censors to intervene. Strange missiles alternated with the flying bouquets, and I looked nervously at the cuspidor beside my desk. It had not yet taken off.

I used my elbows to keep the shouting, milling crowd away from Carmen. I definitely did not want her to have her baby right there at my desk.

"You'd better get out of here," I told her.

She wouldn't budge. Hadn't she earned the right to see the finish? Wasn't she entitled to some return on the chillblains and frozen ears she had suffered on wintry street corners?

My brother Lu and I squeezed through the mob to reach the outside corridor. I needed his counsel. However, the situation was not one envisioned in the Spiritual Exercises of St. Ignatius. For once Lu's finely honed, Jesuit mind couldn't cope. It was Democratic Chairman Jack Dwyer who came up with some practical advice.

"Get the hell across the hall to the registrar's office," he said, "and get yourself sworn in even if you have to blackjack Joe Gallagher."

Joe was the city registrar and a Republican, but he swore us in anyhow.

The tumult and the shouting had subsided somewhat when we returned to the chambers. But Carmen required attention. She was hungry.

There was a break in the bitter controversy so that the aldermen could attend the inauguration ceremonies of the new mayor, but the altercation was resumed afterward without a settlement. The Republicans would not give ground, and the new mayor's inaugural address was put over until the next day.

A committee was finally appointed to resolve the question, but it came to no conclusion for more than two weeks. It was May 6 before Egan and I were allowed to take our seats and admire the lovely cuspidors beside our desks.

As hectic as it was, my entry into public life was a gentle breeze compared to the stormy years that awaited me as mayor of St. Louis.

IV

Dynamite and the Rent Strike

The Tragic Muddle of Public Housing

It was a proud day for St. Louis. The Pruitt-Igoe public housing project was being dedicated. Twenty years had gone by since President Franklin D. Roosevelt called upon his countrymen to correct the shameful statistic that one-third of the nation was ill housed (as well as ill fed and ill clothed). But things were moving at last. The paper promises of the 1930s seemed to be paying off. Here on nearly seventy acres of what had been the most miserable slums of the inner city now stood thirty-two shiny, new high-rise buildings, modern homes for nearly ten thousand souls in the lower-income brackets. The whole nation had reason to take heart.

Architects agreed that the firm of Hellmuth, Yamasaki, and Leinweber of St. Louis and Detroit, winners of the Outstanding Design Award of the American Institute of Architects for another project, had done it again.

The date on which the first family moved into this repository of glowing hopes was October 11, 1954.

Ten years later, Pruitt-Igoe was a shambles. The rows of gleaming windows were mostly dark, jagged-mouth caves now. A few of the broken windows were boarded up to keep out the cold for the tenants who remained. The halls had the reek of a sharecropper's outhouse, and for good reason: they were embellished with deposits of human feces. The thousands of vacant apartments had been stripped by vandals almost before their ex-occupants' meager belongings were on the rented truck. Plumbing was ripped out. Pipes were sold for the metal. Copper was torn from the roof, and bathtubs were broken up to be sold for junk. Toilet bowls were pried from the floor and the water from the attached pipes left to flood the lower floors. The laundry rooms were a mess. The public rooms and mail racks were veritable rats' nests. The architectural gem had become a ghost town haunted by muggers.

Late in the winter of 1968-69 when pipes froze, furnaces broke down, and the wind from the Mississippi howled through broken windows, the notorious rent strike hit Pruitt-Igoe and other St. Louis public-housing units. The strikers' claims were not without some justice, as we shall see later. But deprived of several hundred thousand dollars in rent money, the St. Louis Housing Authority could not make necessary repairs. The vicious circle continued, the impossible problem continued to chase its tail, while argument—not always dialogue—went on between St. Louis and Washington.

Our own people thought Pruitt-Igoe was too far gone to be rehabilitated and recommended tearing the place down and starting over. Secretary George Romney of Housing and Urban Development disagreed. After all, there were $33 million in federal funds tied up in Pruitt-Igoe. He could not see all that money go up in smoke. The sorry state of affairs, said Romney, was due to local mismanagement. We had made the mess; we should clean it up as best we could.

After much bitter correspondence and several trips to Washington, we finally got permission from HUD to blow up two of the units to make room for park and recreation areas.

The dynamiting of two of Pruitt-Igoe's once-lovely, eleven-story buildings was a sensation seen on television and in newspapers and magazines throughout the world. The first charges were laid in March, 1972, and more explosions followed in May and June. The demolition experts we brought in were experimenting with several new techniques. For one building they proved they could destroy the two wings separately without damaging the center section. With the other building they reversed the process. They also succeeded in dynamiting the top floors while leaving the lower stories intact. This type of selective destruction would fit in with the plans we had for future remodeling of Pruitt-Igoe.

When the demolition crews had packed up their explosives and gone home, we were left with two monumental heaps of rubble where the proud buildings once stood.

Summer passed and autumn leaves were beginning to turn. The playgrounds and parks had not left the drawing board, and the rats in the rubble were thriving and multiplying. Secretary Romney accused St. Louis of stalling, apparently unaware of the reams of correspondence that had been exchanged. Interoffice communications, it would seem, were not at their best in this department, and our requests had, as so often happens in a complex bureaucracy, fallen between two stools. Finally, after desperate letters from my office and from Frank E. Boykin, chairman of the St. Louis Housing Authority, HUD authorized the expenditure of $50,000 to chase the rats and reduce the debris heaps to landscaping dimensions, plus about $300,000 for "remedial work" that would make living conditions at least bearable for the remaining six hundred tenants—all black now—during the winter of 1972-73.

When news came through that the federal funds were available at last, I went out to Pruitt-Igoe to make the announcement in person. After making so many promises for so long in the name of the city, I felt that I owed it to the tenants to let them hear the good news—it was moderately good—from the mayor himself. Even so, I am not sure they really believed me.

Approaching Pruitt-Igoe through the early October dusk, I was touched to see a few lighted windows glowing in the desolate acres of dark, glassless casements—tenants who had stayed on because they had no other place to go. The community auditorium was crowded with perspiring, unhappy tenants. It was an unusually warm evening for October, and the air conditioning had long been on the fritz. The words from the floor were hot, too.

After I made my announcement there was a torrent of black oratory. If there was any applause when I said the money was here at last, it was lost in the din of people demanding the microphone and the shrill voices of pig-tailed toddlers playing on the stage, dodging the feet of the speakers, unconcerned with what was going on about them. The

discussion was rarely on target. The usual gripes were aired by men and
women alike, delighted to have the mayor as a captive audience. About
the only speaker who made sense was a man in a red turtleneck sweater
who told the crowd that they were damn fools to pay attention to
promises.

"The white community ain't going to do nothing for you," he
argued. "Nobody's going to do anything for you. You want something
done you gotta do it yourself."

On my way to the car I was waylaid by a voluble woman in green
who had been the loudest and most insistent in her denunciation of the
mayor. She grinned as she reached for my hand and shook it. "I guess I
told 'em, didn't I, Mr. Mayor?" she said. "Did you hear me telling
'em?"

Driving home that night Bill Jud, my chauffeur and discreet eaves-
dropper, reported on what he had gleaned on the fringes of the
assemblage. "Listening around," he said, "I gathered that you didn't go
over very big. They still think that whatever you say is just talk. You
wasted an evening."

I disagreed with Bill. This had been the tenants' night to howl, their
chance to sound off, to air their beefs. It gave them a lift to talk back
to the mayor. Sounding off may not be much help for faulty plumbing
or stalled elevators but it does generate a communal feeling.

II

What happened to cause the bright new slum replacement that was
Pruitt-Igoe to deteriorate spectacularly into an even worse slum over
relatively few years? Who is to blame for the tragic failure? Or is
Pruitt-Igoe more or less typical of the way the public-housing program
has been stumbling along nationally? Before trying to answer these
questions, let's take a quick look at how the program has been taking
shape since President Roosevelt's "one-third of the nation" speech.

I believe I can say without fear of contradiction that the 1937
promise of Congress to provide decent, safe, and sanitary housing for all
the people of the nation has not been kept. World War II interfered, of
course, but the program did not gain momentum until the second
Truman administration. It was 1949 before Congress passed a housing
act declaring that federal aid for slum clearance and low-rent housing

was a matter of national policy. During the Eisenhower regime (1954) Congress voted to provide thirty-five thousand units for families displaced by federal slum clearance. Five years later another housing act authorized the expenditure of $1 billion over two years for slum clearance and housing. In 1963, President Kennedy by executive order directed all federal agencies to eliminate racial or religious discrimination in housing projects built with government assistance.

The problem of the cities did not seem important enough to warrant cabinet stature until 1965, when the Department of Housing and Urban Development was established. By that time Pruitt-Igoe had already reached the lower depths. Why? I think the blame can be pretty evenly divided. Mistakes were made—and are still being made—on all levels of government—local, state and municipal. Some are primary mistakes in concept and planning, such as placing families with small children in high-rises, some are due to bureaucratic rigidity and inertia, and too many are caused by failure of communication between levels of government.

On the federal level there are primary mistakes by the planners and builders. Because Pruitt-Igoe was designed for low-rent occupancy, eleven-story buildings were erected to house the most people possible per square yard. Although there was a saving on land value per tenant, the resulting density of people per unit decreased sharply the available open space for playgrounds and recreation. Experts have determined that when low-income families with children are involved (and they have been at Pruitt-Igoe to an explosive degree), the number of dwelling units per acre should not exceed fifty. Furthermore, high-rise buildings foster anonymity among the occupants, destroying the community feeling that is essential to projects of this type.

The need to keep building costs low led to cutting corners and the use of less expensive materials. Pipes were left unprotected to freeze in winter. Elevators stopped only at every other floor, leaving the tenants of apartments on the skipped floors vulnerable to muggers and rapists lurking in stairwells. The buildings were wide open to outside prowlers. No toilets were provided on ground floors for the convenience of children caught short while playing outside and unable (or unwilling) to get home to the upper floors in time. Result: stinking, unhygienic hallways.

The most serious of shortcomings on a local level was the failure of the St. Louis Housing Authority to do a commonsense job of allocating space in Pruitt-Igoe. I don't mean that there should be an arbitrary screening out of one class or another, but a modicum of integration— not only of races but of ages, income levels, and backgrounds such as the authority had in mind when the complex was opened—is the only basis which had any chance of success. When the authority began increasingly placing welfare families in Pruitt-Igoe, the low-income whites moved out, and the tenant population became entirely black. Moreover, the welfare families were usually overloaded by fatherless households with five or six children apiece. That was why they were on welfare. Of the eight thousand-plus occupants during the first years of Pruitt-Igoe, only twelve hundred were men.

I don't think it is too much to expect that there will some day be intelligent cooperation between local and federal agencies. There is no doubt in my mind that basic responsibility for the problems of the inner city, particularly those of public housing, belongs in Washington. The drift of low-income populations from the rural south to the urban areas is certainly a matter of national dimensions, yet the nuts-and-bolts solution of the problems the drift creates rests with the city. The mechanization of agriculture, the disappearance of the small farm, the growing use of synthetic fibers in place of cotton, factors which have driven the field hand across state lines to industrial centers in search of a livelihood, are surely problems for the federal government. Yet providing that livelihood and reeducating people who are strangers to indoor plumbing, garbage disposal, the telephone, and other habits and conveniences peculiar to the city must be borne locally.

Washington has felt in the past that, having furnished funds for trying to solve these problems, it is entitled to specify the details of how they are to be spent. Still, local conditions vary from place to place, and the regulations laid down by a central bureaucracy are usually too narrow to accommodate regional differences. Public officials, particularly in the lower echelons, have found that they never get in trouble with superiors by saying no. If there is any question about the perils attendant to saying yes, the buck is passed to the next level. Sometimes it gets stuck between levels. Consequently, in matters concerning public housing, Washington too often appears as an absentee landlord. But it's the rent collector—in St. Louis the housing authority

—who gets the blame. And it's the mayor who appoints the housing director who ends up as the villain of the piece.

As an example of strangulation by federal guidelines, let's take "the hot-dog audit."

In the mid-1960s, St. Louis Housing Authority Director Irvin Dagen was looking for ways to improve rapport between public-housing tenants and the authority. He started a series of Sunday afternoon get-togethers in the projects. The authority bought the hot dogs, buns, and soft drinks, while the women in each project cooked the sausages and served the soda.

The program was a big success. Hundreds of tenants engaged in weekly rap sessions—frank but cordial—with the authority staff, chewing over their grievances. For the first time the residents felt they could talk *to* rather than *at* their "landlords." Furthermore, they were getting some response. The informal, social nature of the hot-dog afternoons was bringing neighbors together in a community spirit. The program was, we in St. Louis agreed, a solid (if financially minor) investment.

Washington saw it differently. General Accounting Office auditors took a look at the princely sum of twelve hundred dollars, the total cost of the hot-dog Sundays for a year, ruled it an improper expense and disallowed it.

Had ten times the amount been budgeted for a newsletter or similar middle-class instrument of communication, there would have been no quarrel with Washington, although the tenants would probably have thrown away a newsletter or torn it into squares to hang on a nail. They certainly could not talk back to a brochure.

So the program died, and with it died any chance of understanding that might have prevented the rent strike.

III

The notorious St. Louis rent strike began in February, 1969. According to the script, frustration in the ghetto is supposed to boil over only during the long, hot summer, but, surprising as it may seem, the poor also suffer the winter of their discontent. When the cold wind whips through broken windows and freezing rain beats through the holes in the roof, it is not hard to work up indignant animosity against the world.

It is hard for me to put my finger on the bottom causes of the strike as it is to pinpoint the blame for the failure of Pruitt-Igoe, but as mayor I was used to being the whipping boy. Basically, the roots of the strike go deep into the fallacious thinking underlying our approach to public housing. Perhaps the crucial error of all our programs has been the assumption that the poor will take on middle-class values, manners, and behavior patterns when relocated in brand-new quarters of brick and mortar or steel and concrete. Our national public-housing policies since their inception have been directed at the "middle-class poor." The very poor, and they are not all black by any means, are too often excluded or screened out. Frequently a family on the point of working its way out of the sinkhole of poverty is cast out of public housing for failing to meet arbitrary income limitations.

I am glad to be able to say that St. Louis, unlike some other cities, does not close the doors of public housing to the very poor. And despite the fact that Missouri's welfare program matches the lowest levels in America, the very poor continue to come into St. Louis. In all conscience, the city cannot responsibly consign welfare families to the streets, regardless of the shortage of low-income housing. Throughout the 1960s public housing became our sanctuary of last resort.

This policy, for which there seemed to be no alternative, generated a high concentration of the very poorest, most disadvantaged families in such projects as the infamous Pruitt-Igoe, with Darst-Webbe, Cochrane, and Vaughn not far behind. In addition to multiplying social problems within the projects, our open-door policy made the city housing authority heavily dependent upon the Missouri Department of Welfare and its deplorably low payment structure.

Meanwhile maintenance costs were skyrocketing, and the authority, obliged to pay its own way for day-to-day operations, was having a hard time making ends meet. Appeals to state and federal agencies for help in meeting the cost of utilities, materials, and manpower met the same response. "You're on your own. Find some way to balance your books."

The only way to balance the books, the only remaining source of additional revenue, was higher rents.

The decision to raise rents was an agonizing one for the housing authority. In my opinion, the 1968 rates were not high. Compared to public housing rents in other cities they were, in fact, lower. But the Missouri welfare payments were lower too, and about two-thirds of the thirty thousand tenants in all of St. Louis housing projects got all or part of their income from welfare grants. Their average income was about $3,200 a family. Annual rent averaged $768 ($64 a month per family), and took such a bite out of the budget that family heads (usually women) had trouble feeding themselves and children (usually numerous). The elderly were the hardest hit. Old-age assistance came to $80 a month. None of the thirty thousand could really afford a bigger rent bite.

When the authority announced the higher rent schedules late in 1968, the forces which had been smouldering for years burst into flame. I was not exactly surprised. Ten years earlier when I was an alderman from the South Side I had been shocked by a series that the *Globe-Democrat* was running, with headlines warning that the housing projects were "a big headache" which would become bigger when inflation began to be felt. So I had been aware that the tenants had long been chafing under a rigid welfare structure, arbitrary and moralistic rules, faceless management, lack of social, cultural, and commercial facilities to serve their basic needs. I knew that some of the most responsible tenants had moved out to find homes in the shrinking—and decaying—private market. Others who stayed vented their anger by wrecking the buildings or outraging their fellows. They were not fouling their own nests; they were attacking the Establishment indirectly. When I became aware of the increasing ferment, I could not foresee that when the blow-up came Al Cervantes as mayor would be sitting right at the flash point. I could only hope that the new neighborhood organizations that had come to life under the auspices of the War on Poverty would be a force for moderation.

The news of the rent hike spread through the projects by grapevine even before it was officially announced. The secret, intricate system of internal communication developed by the tenants was quicker and more efficient than Ma Bell's latest electronic switchboard. Word of the decision was known instantly. The laundry rooms buzzed. Phones rang in apartments lucky enough to have them. Elevators reverberated with indignant harangue. Meetings were called.

This time, however, the community reaction did not stop at talk.

Frustration crystallized into action through the determination of a small but resolute group with no organizational affiliation, no resources, and no basic plan. All it had was guts, persistence, and leadership.

At the forefront of the leadership was the Reverend Buck Jones. A black graduate of the Yale School of Religion, he was working as a neighborhood organizer at Plymouth House, a center that primarily served the Carr Square housing project. This low-rise complex on the city's North Side was one of the least volatile of areas, a significant characteristic of low-rise housing which I will discuss later.

During the long months of the strike I got to know Buck Jones well, and I respected him more than any other of the leaders. Although he was soft-spoken and reasonable, he never gave an inch when it came to compromising the interests of the people whose lives he was determined to improve.

The Reverend Jones was a small, wiry man who weighed no more than 140 pounds. Always modestly dressed in white shirt, dark suit, and tie, he instinctively shied away from the spotlight that his position attracted. He lived in a white South St. Louis neighborhood far from most of the housing projects.

After the rent increase was announced Buck Jones discussed plans with the tenants he represented. With their approval—he always insisted on citizen participation in decision making—he decided that the residents of Carr Square would strike. Unless the increase was rolled back, his tenants would withhold their rent from the authority and pay it into a bank account to be held in escrow.

The Reverend Jones was dead set against violence and disorder. He was confident that his peaceful strategy would win. Halfway through the nine-month strike he said: "We have the right approach. I see no tangible benefit to be gained by those who advocate disruption and chaos. More than ever I respect Dr. Martin Luther King."

One strike leader who made a sharp contrast to the personality of Buck Jones was Jean King. Mrs. King was a flaming militant, young and attractive, with a truck driver's vocabulary. She spoke (in sentences rich with four-letter words) for the tenants of the South Side complex that included the Darst, Webbe, and Peabody projects. She represented far fewer rent strikers than the Reverend Jones, yet the television cameras found her more photogenic. Her fiery approach made hotter news.

Had the rent rollback been granted early, I believe the strike would have ended with little substantial change in the operation of public housing in St. Louis. But in the first weeks I don't think anyone, not even the tenants themselves, recognized how intense was the frustration of the strikers or how dedicated was their leadership.

As so often happens in protracted negotiations, the initial demands were escalated almost daily. There were no basic ground rules, no mutual recognition of fundamental interests, no clear definition of the issues. Both parties were playing by ear and as voices grew louder ears grew deafer.

Beyond the primary demand of the rent rollback, the tenants were insisting on the following conditions:

—That rents be geared to ability to pay; no more than 25 percent of the income of public assistance tenants.

—Three-year leases instead of a month-to-month basis.

—Addition of tenant members to the board of the housing authority.

—Improvement of general living conditions and a stipulation that the authority "treat tenants as people."

—A moratorium on all lawsuits and evictions filed in connection with the strike.

The authority had started filing eviction suits, thereby hardening the attitude of the strikers. Consequently, I told Director Dagen and his board to cease and desist. The Legal Aid Society, which furnished $150,000 worth of free legal advice, succeeded in blocking what suits had been filed.

My efforts to find out where the rent money was being held in escrow were regarded by the strike leaders as a reflection on their integrity and a trick by the city to start court action to recover the money. Actually I wanted to be assured that a proper accounting system had been set up so that the authority would get the back rent when the strike was settled. I also suspected that a considerable number of tenants who were not paying rent were pocketing it rather than putting it in escrow. I thought the tenants who were still paying rent—and they amounted to nearly two-thirds of the total—were en- titled to know if their neighbors were "free riders" taking advantage of the situation or were actually putting their money in the rent fund. The very survival of the authority, along with its ability to provide heat and light, depended upon ultimately receiving the withheld rent.

Weeks stretched into months and nerves were getting frayed. New demands were made—scores of them. Proposals for meetings were met with counterproposals. The strikers wanted the meetings closed to the press. I insisted on open meetings. Offers of mediation came from the Church Federation, the Health and Welfare Council, and the Human Development Corporation, our St. Louis war-on-poverty agency.

In the community at large, particularly in the suburbs, apathy was rampant.

Then the strike leaders demanded that I fire Irv Dagen, the authority director.

Dagen was not the most diplomatic of men. He was frank to the point of tactlessness. His bluntness caused many people to call him an abrasive personality. He sometimes annoyed me with decisions he made without consulting me. To complicate matters further, he was accused of involvement in an insurance fraud which had nothing to do with the authority.

I refused to make Dagen a scapegoat. He was entitled to his day in court. The court found that he was the victim of another man's hocus-pocus and dismissed charges against him. He continued to play an important part in city government as counsel for the Urban Renewal Agency, but my refusal to deliver his head to Mrs. Jean King and company did nothing to break the deadlock.

At last I called a meeting of community leaders from all sectors of city life. It was an open meeting, and rent strikers packed the hearing room at City Hall. As far as promoting meaningful dialogue was concerned, the meeting was a total disaster. There was a continuous parade of strike leaders to the microphone attacking the housing authority, my administration, and the white Establishment in general. More heat than light was generated, but one clue to a possible settlement emerged, although I didn't recognize it until next day.

One supporter of the strike was Jake McCarthy, an assistant to Harold Gibbons, Teamster Union boss. To great applause, McCarthy grabbed the mike and shouted: "The Teamsters are behind the rent strike 1,000 percent!"

McCarthy would not have made that statement without the approval of Harold Gibbons, and if the strikers had Gibbons behind them, they had real political clout.

Gibbons and I had faced each other eyeball to eyeball across the negotiating table many times while I was reorganizing the Laclede Taxicab Company. He got his foothold in the Teamsters by unionizing the cab drivers, and his rise in the labor movement paralleled my progress in business and politics. He had a great track record in nosing out opponents. Gibbons was not only top banana in the St. Louis local, but was national vice-president of the Teamsters International Brotherhood. Gibbons was riding high. He was not only an expert at calling a strike, he knew how to settle one. We needed his kind of talent.

I wired Gibbons, asking him as a civic leader to undertake to raise one million dollars to keep public housing open. It was not a bluff. Gibbons was truly a leader in the community and was deeply concerned about the kind of people who have to live in housing projects.

We had several meetings. He did not promise to raise a million dollars, but he did commit himself to using his best efforts to settle the strike and improve conditions in the neoslums like Pruitt-Igoe. As a result he became architect of the Civic Housing Alliance, a coalition of rent-strike leaders, businessmen, educators, members of the clergy, professional men—all those necessary to give the effort a broad spectrum of community credibility.

Gibbons was the kind of man who could involve all levels of the city to cut through emotional rhetoric and reduce the basic differences to cold reality. He had the sort of social mobility that enabled him to sit down to lunch at the Missouri Athletic Club with the elite of the business community, and an hour later drink beer in the ghetto with militant neighborhood leaders. He could—and did—bring black firebrand Jean King into the same room with August A. Busch, Jr., a man whose name is attached to many civic and philanthropic interests.

Meanwhile, I was engaged in an angry exchange with Washington. For several years the city of St. Louis and the Department of Housing and Urban Development had been arguing about the division of responsibility between federal and local governments. With the accession of the Nixon administration and the takeover of HUD by George Romney, I had hoped there might be an admission of substantial obligation for living conditions at Pruitt-Igoe and other projects. After all, the buildings had been erected under federal directives, to federal specifications, with federal money, and operated under budget guidelines drawn by a federal agency. The attitude of HUD was still that the problems were local in character and that St. Louis should dig its own way out.

In the fourth month of the strike I tried again. I asked Lawrence M. Cox, Romney's assistant secretary for renewal and assistance, to send a team of housing experts to analyze the situation and make recommendations. Cox sent a team headed by Edgar Ewing, former director of the Baltimore authority. He also sent a letter which slammed the door in my face before it was even ajar. Ewing and his team had not yet looked at Pruitt-Igoe, but Cox had already reached the following conclusions:

—HUD would not approve a deficit budget which our authority had put together to reduce rents and improve service as a means to end the strike.

—The enormous deficit was due to bad management by the city.

—The fiscal problems could be solved by filling the vacancies at Pruitt-Igoe.

. The first thing that Ewing or any other investigator would see on inspection of Pruitt-Igoe was that nobody in his right mind would want to live there—even the poorest of the poor. The decline had been going on for so long that local opinion was almost unanimous that the whole thing should be torn down.

Still I didn't give up. Wayne Millsap, a prominent St. Louis attorney and a friend of Romney's, arranged a meeting with the secretary in Washington.

As we entered Romney's office, my hopes rose for a frank discussion without sound and fury. The former whiz kid of American Motors was sitting at his desk casually attired in a bright, royal-blue golf sweater.

But Mr. Secretary's attitude was not at all casual. I had scarcely taken a seat when he pointed a stern finger at my midriff and declared ex cathedra that public housing problems in St. Louis had been inherited by the Nixon administration, that they were strictly none of his business, and he felt no obligation to bail us out.

Half an hour later we were on our way home. It looked like a long, hot summer for St. Louis. Unless the authority could get its hands on the back rent money—or any money—all utilities would be shut off in two months and the staff fired.

Gibbons, however, reported progress. His Civic Housing Alliance, with its star-studded roster of professional and business people, was gaining the confidence of the strikers. By the time the smell of autumn was in the air and the football Cardinals had taken over Busch stadium from the baseball Cardinals, the terms of a settlement began to be hammered out. By mid-October a solid agreement was in sight.

I had already called a press conference to announce the end of the strike when a last-minute hitch developed. A key clause in the settlement called for the resignation of all incumbent commissioners on the board of the housing authority and the appointment of a new board. One commissioner, Julius Thompson, refused to resign. He was allied with the Steamfitters Union, which was not at all happy over the idea of the Teamsters moving in on the public housing situation in St. Louis. It took all my energy and ingenuity and all the outside pressure I could muster to get his resignation. But it was secure in my pocket by the time the reporters, the television cameras, the luminaries of the alliance, and the strikers in full battle dress filed into my office.

It was a tense moment. The silence was broken only by the muttering of the camera crews maneuvering for position and the shifting of chairs. I was about to clear my throat and formally open the conference when the Teamsters attorney edged up to my desk and murmured that there was one more little matter that would have to be taken care of before we could begin. As I had no hint of what Harold Gibbons had up his sleeve now, I preferred not to find out in full view of the cameras.

We stepped into the adjoining board room where the Teamsters attorney produced a document which he placed on the table with a flourish. "We'd like your signature," he said.

I took one look at the paper and shook my head. Gibbons was asking me to sign away my authority as mayor to appoint commissioners to the board of the authority. That power, the document read, was henceforth to be vested in the Civic Housing Alliance—in other words, Harold Gibbons. I looked the lawyer straight in the eye.

"I can't sign that," I told him.

It was the simple truth. I could not sign away a power that had been conveyed by law to the mayor. I couldn't sign away the last small measure of accountability that the public had the right to demand of an elected official.

The attorney said nothing, but he gave me a cynical smile which seemed to say, "Come on Mayor, don't stall. You know Hal Gibbons has got you up a tree and if you try to jump down you'll land astride a picket fence. . . ."

"I'm not going to sign," I repeated quietly.

The attorney shrugged. "It's either-or," he said. "No signature, no deal."

Gibbons' shrewd, gutsy move had me in a tight corner. He had held off playing his joker until the crowd had gathered to hear my announcement of the settlement.

"Then it's no deal," I said.

The attorney shrugged again and picked up the unsigned document. There was a sadistic gleam in his eye as he watched me stalk back to face the press and tell the crowd there was no settlement after all. Halloween was just around the corner and who would be the leading candidate for hobgoblin of the year?

Mayor Al Cervantes. Who else?

I gave them the bad news as concisely as possible. The strikers had apparently been tipped off; they were the first to reach the exits. As the others filed out, puzzled and disappointed, I heard my name muttered with some epithets I have tried to forget. The television lights were still glaring at me. I must have looked pretty grim.

Chris Condon, the TV newsman for Channel 5, volunteered: "You're playing a pretty steep game of poker, aren't you, Mayor?"

"I'm not sure of the name of the game," I replied, "but whatever it is, there's no other way for me to play it."

Mine was apparently the right way because later that day I had a phone call from Gibbons's office. There must be some way to work this thing out, said a spokesman for the Teamsters. And sure enough, there was, and without any or-else ultimatums. Lawyers for both sides sat down and, as only lawyers can, found the appropriate language to cloak all parties with a modicum of sanity and a vestige of reason.

The second press conference was an anticlimax but it marked the end of the strike after nine months—a period of gestation that had brought forth hard feelings, wasted energy, results which should have been accomplished in weeks, and a total of $729,000 owed to the housing authority.

The strikers did win the rent limit of 25 percent of income, a real victory, a reasonable concession, and a ratio that may prove to be a revolutionary precedent.

A new tenant-participation structure was created, with residents given a substantially stronger voice in management. Plans were laid for a tenant corporation that may eventually operate some of the projects.

A new board took over management of the housing authority and somehow established better rapport with the federal agencies so that subsidies and grants began to come in. New federal legislation was enacted to provide support to local housing authorities in trouble— indubitably a logical sequel to the strike.

Best of all, a major catastrophe had been averted, and incidentally a cruel political cross had been lifted from my shoulders. Under the circumstances I didn't mind being designated the loser by the media.

Actually there were no winners. Despite the lower rents, vacancy rates continued to rise. Pruitt-Igoe continued to be an ill-kept pigsty. The civic alliance set its top professionals to surveying the blighted buildings and came to the conclusion that they were indeed doomed. To put the buildings back in repair would cost more than $28 million. It would be better to tear the whole damned thing down and start over.

The conclusion to raze Pruitt-Igoe was not reached in a vacuum. Washington had been consulted and kept abreast of all stages of the deliberation. One of Romney's top aides, the Reverend Kirk Walsh, S.J., was apprised of the recommendation to dynamite, and although he saw the political drawbacks, he realized its realistic necessity.

It was at this point that Secretary Romney made his trip to St. Louis for a first-hand look. As we watched his snappy Lear jet taxi down the runway at Lambert Field we dared be optimistic. Now that the secretary would be seeing for himself what we were up against, maybe we could expect understanding and help from Washington.

Romney showed sympathetic interest as we toured the ruined project. He was more than cordial during a pleasant luncheon. We seemed to be talking the same language at last.

Then we returned to my office where Congresswoman Lenore Sullivan opened the briefing. It was Terrence McCormick, one of the Teamster experts studying the Pruitt-Igoe situation, who zeroed in on the $64 million question. He explained why the only logical answer to

Pruitt-Igoe was to tear it down and start from scratch with what we had learned from everybody's costly errors.

"Nonsense!" said Mr. Secretary, and we were back where we started. "The project must be rehabilitated. It just can't be torn down. You people should get greater involvement from the private sector of your community."

I pointed out that the civic alliance represented all levels of private enterprise in St. Louis and was deeply involved in the problems of public housing.

Romney shook his head. There was the little matter of bonded indebtedness, something like $30 million of government-backed paper.

I reminded Mr. Secretary that the government had liquidated other bonds.

The meeting was not a total loss. Romney did promise closer cooperation with "our people." We did finally get HUD's permission to dynamite two units of Pruitt-Igoe even if it did take months to remove the rat-ridden debris and start landscaping the area of the ruins. And we did get an appropriation to ameliorate the frightful conditions of the few hundred tenants still imprisoned in Pruitt-Igoe. But the ultimate solution is still a long way off.*

George Romney is a capable, dedicated man with all the good will in the world. President Nixon accepted his resignation at the beginning of his second term. Whether he left HUD because his own projected program clashed with the President's political strategy of coddling the white suburbs at the expense of the inner cities, or whether he gave up trying to deal with problems of such frustrating dimensions I do not know. But I do know that the problems are still pregnant with terrible danger.

I also know that America should be able to tell its citizens that they will have decent homes by the end of the 1970s, as they were promised in 1937. I know that we must remove the suburban noose from around the neck of our black inner-city dwellers. I know that we must have

---

*As this book goes to press, both local and federal authorities have definitely given up on Pruitt-Igoe. The last tenant moved out on May 4, 1974, and a seven-foot fence was erected to keep the vandals from a final spree.

closer cooperation between all levels of government and all levels of society.

It is on the lack of this cooperation that I lay the blame for the tragedy of Pruitt-Igoe. The minor local inefficiencies upon which Washington tried to saddle the blame were merely contributing factors. The foundations of quicksand leading to the collapse of the project were laid in Washington.

The U.S. Housing Act of 1949 (as modified) set the guildelines which forced the use of inferior materials in order to meet cost specifications. The price limitations fixed by Congress made necessary the exposed pipes, the skip-a-floor elevators, the lack of toilets on the ground floor. The use of land requirements forced the crowded units to be built without park or recreation areas. It was federal guidelines that set rents on a nationwide basis with no regard for differential between state welfare allowances. Given the low welfare grants by the state of Missouri, the Washington-fixed rentals often absorbed all but 25 percent of the available income of a Pruitt-Igoe tenant. A sympathetic attempt at understanding instead of a bureaucratic deaf ear would have spared us much grief.

I am not reckless enough to pretend that St. Louis has all the answers, but I think we have been taking a few short steps in the right direction.

V

America Needs a Commitment

Wanted: 26 Million New Dwellings

Unless we are satisfied to have our socioeconomic clock turned back far beyond the New Deal, beyond the Hoovervilles, back at least as far as the laissez-faire years of the McKinley era, we are going to have to build before the end of this century more housing than has been built over the entire existence of the United States. As a start we must provide at least 26 million additional housing units before the end of the 1970s. In fact, we will be building a second America.

Will the cities of this second America be left with rotting cores and festering slums? During the two decades preceding the seventies, only half a million housing units were built for the disadvantaged, and the problem is still not being faced realistically. On the eve of stepping down from his post as secretary of Housing and Urban Development, George Romney admitted (not surprisingly) that his public housing program had been a failure, and that the federal government should get out of the public housing field and leave it to the states, which are in a better position to handle the problem.

Mr. Romney is right in saying that the program has been generally a failure, but he is wrong in his desire to give responsibility to the states. The financial burden must remain essentially with the national authority, but shifting the planning and administration to the states instead of to the cities would be worse in some ways than leaving them in Washington. State legislatures are usually heavily dominated by conservative rural representatives who view the cities as sources of crime and iniquity unworthy of any help that interferes with funds earmarked for stabilizing farm prices or social purposes above the county level.

The cities are best fitted to cope with housing problems because they are intimately involved. Still, they are unable to bear the financial burden because of diminishing tax bases due to the migration of business and individual taxpayers to the lily-white suburbs. Yet to say the city is in the front line is not enough. The city must be involved in all socioeconomic and ethnic levels, much as we involved St. Louis business, labor, government, professional men, educators, and religious leaders in the final solution of our rent strike—the civic alliance. And just as all levels are involved in our "Challenge of the Seventies" plan.

One example of how private enterprise became involved in providing low- and moderate-cost housing is the LaSalle Park Urban Renewal Project, which came off the drawing boards in the fall of 1972. LaSalle Park is a slum region just south of the central business section of St. Louis declared a "blighted area" by the city in 1969. While some industries have been moving out of the central city, the Ralston Purina Company is putting up $2 million to implement a plan already drawn jointly by Ralston's architects and the city Development Authority.

The dilapidated old buildings—residential, commercial and industrial —were in 1972 either vacant, rundown, or vandalized, or all three. The redevelopment program calls for a new viable community of homes for low- and moderate-income families, stores and shops, as well as institutions such as churches.

When I first discussed this project with R. H. Dean, chairman of the board of Ralston, Alderman Leisure of the ward containing LaSalle Park, and Charles F. Farris, director of the city's Land Clearance for Redevelopment Authority, the area involved comprised nearly 150 acres. Plans were drawn for the development of this area to include six hundred units especially for the elderly, but HUD informed us that the federal funds needed to complement Ralston's offer of $6 million were not available under the Neighborhood Development Program.

In 1969, however, we managed to cut through the various bureaucratic objections and get funds committed for one-third the original area—forty-four acres. Ralston put up $2 million against $6 million of federal money. The total "net project cost" included the cost of land, relocating the tenants of the condemned slums, tearing down the squalid rat-invaded buildings, grading new streets, landscaping, etc.

The approved plans have been based on critical analysis of the desolate Pruitt-Igoe fiasco. In accordance with the guidelines of the 1968 Federal Housing Act, there were to be no high-rise buildings for families with children. Two- and three-story walkups are designed to contain 112 townhouses and 36 garden apartments, the latter to occupy the ground floors of the three-story buildings. The plans include two "tot lots" with appropriate play equipment and well-planted common areas. Apartments would rent for $60 to $100 and occupancy would be limited to families below the $6,000 to $9,000 income range. Tenancy would of course be integrated and provision made for tenants to become owners.

The ethnic and sociological profile of the neighborhood is being preserved. Six churches are still active in LaSalle Park, reflecting the German, Lebanese, Czech, and Bohemian character of the area in the last century. The Lebanese who came to St. Louis in the 1800s brought with them the Maronite rite of the Catholic church, and their descendants who are keeping the original St. Raymond's church alive plan to build a new Maronite church of oriental architecture for the "new town in town." Other existing churches—Lutheran, Baptists, Presbyterians, Roman Catholics—are also cooperating.

The LaSalle Park project is particularly dear to my heart because it exemplifies my current philosophy: that the scandalous plight of the cities can be solved only by the cooperation of business and industry whose own future is tied willy-nilly to the fate of urban survival. I am hopeful that the example of Ralston Purina will inspire other corporations whose past has been part of the life of St. Louis to realize their responsibility to contribute to the rebirth of the city they considered abandoning. In the words of R. Hal Dean, chairman of the board of Ralston Purina, "We hope that our efforts will serve as a catalyst for others in the private sector to become involved in the rebuilding of our city."

II

Another example of cooperation between the private sector and federal financing became a going concern during the agony of Pruitt-Igoe.

In 1960 the Mill Creek Valley neighborhood of St. Louis was a shameful slum with an appalling juvenile delinquency rate, the usual decaying buildings, a thriving rat population, high incidence of tuberculosis, and statistics on armed robbery and drug addiction that raised the hackles of even the hardened police of the Ninth District.

By 1965 Mill Creek Valley had become the site of Laclede Town, composed of 300-row houses built with $4 million of federally insured mortgage money obtained under Section 221-D (3) of the 1961 Federal Housing Act. The private sector was represented here by the St. Louis firm of Millstone Construction Co., contractors, and the then-New York Congressman James H. Scheuer. The two- and three-story houses are not for the destitute-level poor, but they rent for limits set by FHA for low-to-moderate income families. To qualify for the lowest rentals ($80), tenants must not earn more than $6,300 a year.

Five years after the first family moved in, there were 669 units and 3,000 residents on the 28-acre tract, and the ultimate figures will be at least 1,700 units and 6,000 residents—if the FHA money does not dry up during the second Nixon administration.

Besides FHA limits on rentals and incomes, private builders' profits must be held to 6 percent, and management fees cannot exceed 3 percent of gross receipts. However, in addition to low-interest mortgages, Laclede Town profits by local tax advantages: for the first ten years taxes are levied only on the assessed value of the land before the project was built; for the next fifteen years buildings and improvements pay taxes on half the assessed rate.

Architecturally, Laclede Town is surprisingly attractive. Designed by Clothiel Smith of Washington with an assist from Leo A. Daley of St. Louis, the row houses are built in thirty-nine different styles, varying roof lines and facades, with alternating frame and varicolored brick. It is a low-density project with only thirty units per acre. There are certain communal amenities (swimming pool, play areas, laundromats, etc.) and strict attention has been paid to the principles of what the modern city planners like Oscar Newman call "defensible space." This planning has paid off. In the early 1970s the crime rate in Laclede Town was the lowest in the still-troubled Ninth Police District. Women are no longer afraid to walk in the streets there.

The tenants of Laclede Town present a broad spectrum. More than 30 percent are black. Many are students and instructors from nearby colleges. Other are truck drivers and physicists, waiters and engineers, policemen and black militants, folk singers, musicians, and military men. One is an ecdysiast—a strip teaser; she lives next door to a minister. Laclede Town's single church—the Berea Presbyterian—is a holdover from the old slum. Built at the turn of the century, it was formerly an all-black congregation. It is now integrated in reverse.

The very poor will not benefit much from such projects as Laclede Town and LaSalle Park unless the idea of housing allowances gains more momentum, which is not likely during the second Nixon administration. Such allowances would go directly to the disadvantaged who would seek their own housing—if any—without the hurdles of the middlemen.*

The very-low-income tenants could benefit if "Operation Breakthrough," originated by Secretary Romney, ever reaches full fruition. St. Louis was one of the 9 cities chosen from among 218 sites proposed for the breakthrough experiment, which was intended to apply the advantages of low-cost, mass-produced techniques to the housing industry and dramatically increase the supply of dwellings. Romney felt that building costs were kept too high by fragmented local construction industries beset by underfinanced small contractors, lopsided building codes, and jealousies between craft unions.

To break through these cost-raising barriers and bring decent housing within reach of people in the lower-income brackets, Romney invited bids on a world-wide basis for producers of what HUD calls "housing systems"—prefabricated houses and units made by assembly-line methods. From more than two hundred competitors, twenty-two firms

---

*On May 10, 1974, President Nixon announced an emergency program allocating up to $10.3-billion extra mortgage money at bargain interest rates to spur the slack private housing market. None of it was earmarked for low-income housing.

were chosen to produce some three thousand prototypes in housing systems, ranging from precast concrete or wood-framed modules to metal or plastic units, and assemblies of prefabricated slabs—floors; walls and ceilings. At an optimistic moment before he resigned in disillusionment, Romney predicted that by 1980 two-thirds of American housing would either be factory built or use prefabricated units.

For St. Louis's share in Operation Breakthrough, some fifteen acres were cleared from the same Mill Creek Valley slum area that produced Laclede Town. HUD chose as housing systems producers Descon-Concordia, Ltd., of Montreal with subsidiaries in several U.S. cities, and Rouse-Wates, a London firm with a branch in Maryland. Plans called for 463 units.

When the time came for us to implement the city's part in the experiment, all the obstacles that Romney blamed for overpriced housing arose to block us. The board of aldermen balked, largely because of pressure from both builders and union leaders. It took all the persuasiveness I could muster to convince the city fathers that Operation Breakthrough would be good for St. Louis as well as the nation.

Both contractors and unions were unhappy over the fact that practically all the work but the final installation would be done off-premises. Prefabricated rooms are delivered as modules to be piled atop each other or connected in tandem or in clusters. Walls, roofs, and floors come as slabs. Plastic pipes are already in place and need only to be connected to the mains. Wiring has been done at the factory. Foundations are precast so there is no local masonry required. It is not surprising that plumbers, steamfitters, electricians, and bricklayers have been unhappy, and that their unhappiness was forcefully conveyed to the board of aldermen.

Pressure by the unions is hard for a politician to resist, but we managed by a few votes to overcome the labor lobbyists' objections. In fact, the unions were beginning to face the problem on a national basis and began signing contracts with the housing-systems producer at his factories. When we got the board to lift all zoning and building-code restrictions which interfered with mass-produced housing, St. Louis could say to HUD: Here's the land; get on with the experiment.

Operation Breakthrough is not a public-housing project, although we expect to have some low-income tenants on a rent-supplement basis to help create the socioeconomic mix that is working so well in Laclede Town, and which we expect to work in LaSalle Park also. Skillful management would bring people from all walks of life and form another integrated community within the larger community which is a changing St. Louis.

However, frankly, the Breakthrough program in St. Louis is drastically behind schedule.

On a nationwide basis, Operation Breakthrough is not living up to Romney's expectations. Some of the producers of modular systems have dropped out of the experiment, because transportation problems, among others, have proved too expensive to be solved on a short-term basis. However, national sales figures of modules continue to climb at the rate of 50 percent a year—120,000 homes in 1972—and mass-production advocates continue to believe that the surviving firms are riding a wave of the future.

III

During most of that October day, I had been in discussion with black groups, and the housing problem was of course high on the agenda. While I was in the midst of an argument with a caucus of black aldermen, Dick McGee, my administrative assistant, came into my office to murmur in one ear that there were a dozen Negro tots, none older than eight or nine, parading up and down the sixty-foot length of the reception hall, taking turns at opening the door to my anteroom and shouting in piping voices, "Mayor, come out! Mayor, come out!" As my own office is more than fifty feet long, I hadn't heart them.

I asked Dick to handle the situation the best he could until I had finished with the aldermen, who were engaged in some agile logrolling. They had heard that the St. Louis portion of federal revenue sharing was about to be paid to the city, and each alderman wanted his share of the reputed millions for neighborhood projects in his own ward, particularly for improving housing. In return for special consideration in the allocation of the manna from Washington, the black aldermen would support a measure I was anxious to have passed by the board—a referendum for building a much-needed convention center for the city.

While I was trying to explain the priorities I would have to set in distributing the federal money, Dick McGee was back to report that the moppets were still marching and screaming, "Mayor, come out!" He said that their mothers and a delegation of neighbors were also waiting in the reception hall, and that television crews had just arrived.

I told Dick to try and hold the fort a little longer. I was not even supposed to be at City Hall that week. I had been in Europe to address the fall session of the Chief Executives Forum and had come back a few days early for the sole and specific purpose of receiving a report that I hoped would resolve a difficulty that had been rankling in several sectors for some years.

During my first months as mayor I expanded and reorganized the Council on Human Relations to deal with cases of discrimination against black St. Louisans. The council's purpose was to get whites to understand racial prejudice from the black point of view and to meet head-on specific cases of discrimination in housing, employment, and the thousand-and-one ways in which blacks have been treated unjustly for years. The council had been trying to generate a harmonious way of life, to persuade by cajolery whites who were guilty of refusing to rent houses or apartments to Negroes, or to bar them from jobs. When persuasion failed, the council would crack down legally on offenders.

My choice as chief commissioner had been Andrew J. Brown, Jr., who happened to be white. It was my feeling that inasmuch as the council would be confronting whites almost exclusively, a white man would be the logical appointment. A vocal black minority of the council disagreed—for political reasons, I am convinced—and carried their disagreement to the point of an anti-Cervantes feud. They wanted a black chairman and in fact had a candidate ready to accept the job and the comfortable emolument that went with it.

Their demand that I fire Andy Brown went on for years and became quite bitter—pickets, press conferences, televised protests claiming that Mayor Cervantes had appointed a racist to head the commission to combat racism. I still refused to fire Andy Brown, but it was obvious that I had to do something to defuse this ticking time-bomb that could destroy the Council on Human Relations, or at least its purpose. So I got together a nationwide panel of civil rights leaders whose integrity was unquestioned—black VIPs from places like Seattle, Dallas, Kansas

City, chaired by Arthur L. Green of Hartford, Connecticut—to review objectively the work of my St. Louis commission and determine whether there was any evidence of discrimination, dereliction of duty, or political hanky-panky that would justify my dismissal of Chairman Brown.

The Green report had been distributed during my absence in Europe, and I had come back ahead of schedule to hear the council members discuss it. The report found that the St. Louis council had been doing a generally satisfactory job, and the council members, despite the dissident minority, agreed to accept the gentle pat on the back.

The group of black aldermen whose meeting had followed that of the council were not as agreeable. As they lingered on to argue, I excused myself to go out and meet the juvenile lobbyists, their fond mamas, and their concerned neighbors for the benefit of the television cameras.

The mothers were two sisters, and the ten children were divided equally between them. Their husbands had disappeared without leaving a forwarding address, and both sisters were on relief. They had been ordered out of their slum apartment as the building was being torn down to make way for an urban renewal project. They had refused to move, understandably, until quarters had been found large enough to hold a household of ten children and two adults. Meanwhile, the electricity and water had been shut off in the condemned building. The sisters bought candles and, with the help of friends, carried water from a block away in pots, pans, and empty bottles. They had come to City Hall in desperation. What was the mayor going to do about it?

The mayor knew that suitable living space was not just around the corner, even for a less numerous household, but the ladies were certainly entitled to more prompt service from the city. I would find out where the laxity was that allowed the situation to reach this point, but I was not going to accede to their demand to be moved into a hotel that very night, even with the TV cameras looking on. Once a dependent family gets settled in a hotel, nothing short of dynamite or a bulldozer can move them into less convenient quarters. However, I did promise them that they would be out of their condemned building by noon next day.

Their personal appeal to the mayor (with a tip-off to the electronic media) was not overdramatizing the housing shortage that St. Louis, like all big cities, is suffering. The housing problems of the rock-bottom poor and the impecunious elderly are not going to be immediately solved by the success of Laclede Town or the promise of Operation Breakthrough and LaSalle Park. However, all of these projects have learned from the deplorable mistakes of Pruitt-Igoe. And what we have learned will make for a brighter future for public housing.

Even Washington seems on the point of giving up the idea of imposing institutionalized features on housing projects coast-to-coast. The advice of behavioral scientists is being heeded in the gradual abandonment of such dehumanizing factors as county-hospital-type white-tiled walls in the corridors. Anything which debases the tenant, or gives the impression of keeping the poor in their proper places, invites vandalism. The row houses and small-unit walkups engender a feeling of ownership, of the tenant being in his own home, even though on relief, and thereby encourage care and neatness.

HUD is even adopting some of the guidelines of Oscar Newman, director of New York University's Institute of Planning and Housing, who was one of the experts studying the disaster of Pruitt-Igoe. Newman found that smaller living space gave the tenant a feeling of "territoriality," a sense of pride and responsibility for a specific area.* Even in the shambles that was Pruitt-Igoe during his survey, he found areas on many floors where two apartments separated by a fire door from the rest of the corridor boasted spotless floors and a feeling of ownership. Six families on one corridor should be the maximum; beyond that, the impression of territoriality vanishes, the sense of community responsibility diminishes, and the rate of crime and vandalism soars.

Design of living space, Newman found, was a more critical factor in crime incidence than the density of occupancy. The crime rate in high-rise projects, he says, are two and three times higher than in low-rise walkups with the same social profile of tenancy.

Newman's point of "territorial restriction" is borne out by one instance at Pruitt-Igoe. A few years ago, we tried putting up new

*Oscar Newman, *Defensible Space* (New York: Macmillan Co., 1972).

playground equipment and some benches near one building. To forestall theft of materials, the area around the building was fenced off, except for a gate opposite the main entrance. When the construction was finished six months later, the tenants asked that the fence be retained. The crime and vandalism rate in that building had dropped to 80 percent of the Pruitt-Igoe average. It was the only unit in Pruitt-Igoe still 90 percent occupied (the overall average was less than 30 percent) and where the tenants kept the halls clean.

It is encouraging that some attention is at last being paid to the human element in urban renewal. In fact, urban renewal should be subdivided into physical and social renewal. We are making some progress with the physical—the bulldozing of antediluvian hovels, the landscaping, the erection of decent dwellings—and it is certainly of utmost importance. But we have been neglecting the social.

Cities disintegrate socially as well as physically. Urban blight is social as well as physical. We know the symptoms: prejudice, hatred, rioting, juvenile delinquency, crime in the streets, alcoholism, dope addiction, broken homes, abandoned children, irresponsibility, lack of pride in self, in the neighborhood, in the city.

Through the years that I occupied City Hall it had been one of my top priorities to muster all the forces available—public and private, civic and social, city, state, and federal—to fight social decay. It is a more difficult battle, because the lines are not drawn in rotting timbers and reeking halls. The enemy is elusive, but he is real.

One of the objectives of our Challenge of the Seventies is St. Louis is a renewal of our human and social values.

VI

No. 1 Priority of the American City

Reduction of Crime on the Street

Crime is more than the annual FBI Uniform Crime Reports.

Crime is more than the figures from the St. Louis police blotter or on the Chicago police blotter or the statistics from the Police Judiciaire on the Quai d'Orsay in Paris.

For the mayor of St. Louis, crime is an old lady whose throat is cut when she resisted the hoodlum trying to snatch her handbag on her way home from the supermarket.

For the mayor, crime is a young social worker mugged, robbed, and raped by two jobless heroin addicts who jumped her in a stairwell while she was walking down one floor (the elevator stopped only at every other floor) to visit a welfare family.

Crime is also a little five-year-old girl lured to the roof with a candy bar by a high-school dropout who abused her sexually and threw her eleven stories to her death when she screamed.

Crime is an old man I met in a hospital elevator. He almost cried on my shoulder. Years ago, he said, he and his wife had bought a little house for seven thousand dollars. The mortgage had been paid off and for some time they had been living on social security. But in the last year or two they had been terrified by several burglaries and face-to-face armed robberies. His wife had had a nervous breakdown and refused to go back and live in the house that represented their life savings. What could he do? He had no money. Nobody would buy his house because it was in a crime-prone neighborhood. He was going to rent a house in suburbia at a rental that would eat up most of his social security. What would happen to him?

Crime is also a drive down Lindell Boulevard, once the swank thoroughfare through middle-class St. Louis. Today it is plastered with "To Rent or Lease" and "For Sale" signs. The Red Cross is moving from its headquarters because its secretaries are afraid to come to work at night. High-rise buildings are vacant for the same reason: fear. Citizens won't park along the street because vandals, if they can't steal the car, will rip off the aerial and slice the tires.

Crime is a 20-story office building that once sold for a million dollars. The neighborhood has deteriorated in the past ten years so that it is an island in a sea of black pool halls and bars. Tenants are moving out. The owner can't give the building away. He is boarding up the property. Why?

Crime is fear.

These are not statistics, but statistics cannot be ignored.

Like all big cities, St. Louis had a frightening increase in crimes against persons and property during the fifties and sixties. In the period from 1952 to 1968, serious crime in St. Louis jumped 206 percent. Auto thefts were twice the national rate. Narcotics arrests doubled for those under twenty-one. More than one-third of those held for major crimes were under seventeen, two-thirds under twenty-one.

Faced with these facts, what does a mayor do?

I studied the sociologists' graphs showing the interrelation of crime with the economic, family, and educational factors of the wrongdoers' backgrounds. I speak from personal experience when I say that there is one factor that cuts across all the rest and outweighs them: the ethnic factor. I myself had one strike against me when I started out on my own. I came from a broken family, but I was lucky enough to have two things going for me. The first was a mother with the strength of character to keep the family together after my father wandered off. The second was that I was not black. If I had been, the chances of my reaching the upper echelons of either business or government—or even of my staying out of jail—would have been stacked against me.

During the first few years I occupied Room 200 in City Hall, I'll admit I was baffled by the curious police setup. The board of police commissioners for St. Louis is appointed by the governor of Missouri, although the money for police salaries comes from city taxpayers. Toward the end of my first term, however, I created a Commission on Crime and Law Enforcement as part of the Challenge of the Seventies plan.

The purpose of this commission was like that of the other sub-systems of the Challenge program—to get officials and citizens in related fields, people who had previously been virtually strangers, to meet on speaking terms, to cross-fertilize ideas, to analyze past errors, and perhaps evolve practical solutions by synthesis and inter-communication. For instance, the official members included the judge of the city's juvenile courts, the presiding judge of the circuit courts, the superintendent of schools, the prosecuting attorney, the circuit attorney, the president of the board of police commissioners, and the president and vice-president of the board of aldermen. The citizens' advisory section of the crime commission included nonsalaried public-spirited experts in fields related to the official members, with added areas such as narcotics, community involvement, and auto thefts.

As executive director of the Commission on Crime and Law Enforcement I had in mind from the first Col. Curtis Broston, retired chief of St. Louis Police, who, in his sixteen years as the city's top cop, had made St. Louis an unhealthy place for organized crime. He had the practical knowledge of the problems of law enforcement from the policeman's viewpoint.

As chairman of the commission I wanted someone who knew the ins-and-outs of the workings of the law courts, with all their defects, someone who had first-hand knowledge of the administration of justice and its relation to the world of crime. The name of the man who it seemed to me could make the greatest positive contribution with his brilliant legal mind was Morris A. Shenker, long St. Louis's outstanding attorney handling criminal cases.

I had known Morris Shenker for some time. Jack Murphy, the young attorney I had retained when I first entered politics, once worked in his office. Before calling Shenker I told some of my staff about my idea of offering him the chairmanship. Opinion was divided. About half of the staff thought I was making a political mistake, in view of Shenker's public image. After all, he had defended some pretty tough characters in court, and while he hadn't been able to keep Jimmy Hoffa, the Teamster boss, out of jail, he had done better for some of the leading racketeers and gamblers in the state. However, he had just the kind of knowledge I thought would be most useful in our long-range effort to reduce crime in the streets. So I called him.

Morris Shenker himself warned me against making the appointment.

"You'd better think it over," he said.

"I have thought it over," I told him, "and you're the man I want."

"Better think some more."

"Okay," I said, "but meanwhile you'd better be thinking, too—about the kind of job you want the commission to do—because my mind's made up."

It was, but to reinforce my own opinion, I consulted the man who was going to be the boss of the professional staff, Colonel Broston.

"A good choice," said the retired police chief. "Shenker is a regular lecturer at the police academy. Both the detectives and uniformed men find him valuable in presenting the legal angles—how to make evidence stand up in court, how to get the sort of identification the defense attorney can't knock down, that kind of thing."

When I got back to Shenker he still shook his head—but he accepted.

"I really can't afford the time, but I'll give you a year, maybe two."

The Commission on Crime and Law Enforcement was formally authorized by the board of aldermen on December 29, 1969, and it went to work immediately.

Fifteen months later Morris Shenker made a progress report to me. The officials of the principal criminal justice agencies had met twenty-seven times, the report read, and the citizen commissioners had met twenty-four times en bloc and at subcommittee meetings more frequently. The report did not mention it, but Chairman Shenker never missed a meeting. Even if he happened to be in New York or on the West Coast on business, he would fly back to St. Louis to preside.

One result of the meetings was an improved relationship between principals of the agencies in understanding each others' problems. At one meeting, for instance, the representative of the juvenile court expressed a need for more prosecutors to clear crowded dockets. On the spot, the circuit attorney and the prosecuting attorney agreed to furnish required personnel. A similar exchange resulted in the criminal court dockets being reduced from more than 1,700 to 1,255 in a single year (1971). Furthermore, the time lag in bringing felony cases to trial, formerly a year or more, was reduced to 4½ months.

During the first year, the commission allotted some $840,000 of federal money to its projects, most of it through the Law Enforcement Assistance Administration (LEAA) of the Justice Department. The funds allowed the commission to get off to a good start. While the FBI's Uniform Crime Reports showed a national increase of major crimes of 11 percent in 1971, St. Louis showed a *decrease* of 3.3 percent. The downward trend continued into the next year. The first quarter of 1972 found the serious crime rate down by 8.6 percent compared to a similar period of 1971.

With all due modesty, I think I can claim credit for some of our success. It was my idea to use some of the LEAA dollars to renew the old-fashioned neighborhood foot patrols, which had pretty much disappeared since the advent of radio-directed police autos. In those neighborhoods where the cop on the beat is again making his sidewalk rounds, major crimes dropped 13.6 percent, burglaries went down 19 percent, and the average of all crimes against persons went down 7.2 percent.

I also reactivated the police horses, most of which had been put out to pasture when it was decided that the internal-combustion engine is mightier than the hayburner. When we put the mounted police to patrolling our 1,400-acre Forest Park, crime dropped off so sharply in the area that we expanded the patrols first to other parks, next to downtown areas and the riverfront. As a result, holdups, rape, armed robbery, and assault fell off a surprising 60 percent in mounted patrol areas.

When the commission began functioning I was shocked to learn that St. Louis had achieved national fame—negatively. Our rate of auto thefts ranked fourth among cities of comparable size, rising 45 percent in 1969, against a national average of 23 percent. We were doing pretty well in 1968 with 11,185—more than 30 a day—but 1969 topped that figure with 14,434. It was obviously time for the light to turn red.

Most cars are stolen because owners leave their keys in the ignition, and for a time the commission considered levying a four-dollar fine for thus encouraging the auto thief. Legislation was actually drafted to this effect. However, techniques of mass persuasion took precedence, and we launched a high-powered campaign in all media instead, using a slogan to remind careless car owners that they should "lock it and pocket the key." That year (1970) car thefts dropped 15 percent and the decrease continued the following year with another 9 percent.

Using the FBI average valuation of $1,200 a car, the first year of implementing the "lock it and pocket the key" program saved the citizens of St. Louis more than $3 million in cars that were not stolen.

First-year projects of the crime commission varied from enlarging the public defender's staff to renovating the city jail and introducing job training at the city workhouse.

Some of the commission's recommendations have resulted in city ordinances, such as one requiring pawnshops to photograph all persons pledging articles of value. Others required the registration of junk and second-hand dealers, aimed at discouraging vandalism for profit.

Another ordinance, designed to increase the responsibility of parents for their juvenile delinquents, provides a fine of up to five hundred dollars for parents of a child under seventeen for "failure to exercise reasonable parental control" when such failure gets the youngster into trouble with the law.

Still another ordinance drawn by the commission provides for the serving of a sentence intermittently upon recommendation to the court by the Director of Welfare. Under certain conditions, the court may allow a prisoner to spend weekdays working at some approved job to support his family, locking him behind bars for every weekend until he has served all his accumulated time. This project ties in neatly with a $100,000 LEAA-funded program for counseling, job training and placement for inmates of the city workhouse. The object of both plans is to reduce recidivism and deter young offenders from a life of crime. St. Louis police statistics show that two-thirds of robbery cases and three-fourths of the burglary arrests are repeaters.

The Police Youth Corps, another long-range program with great potential, was initiated on a pilot basis in two police districts. The project, with the cooperation of both police and fire departments, exposes teen-agers to the workings of the services, gives them some high school courses, and makes them aware of the educational requirements for becoming policemen or firemen, with the attendant advantages. The five hundred youths enrolled in the first year grew to more than one thousand (among them three hundred girls) in 1972. There was a waiting list of another thousand who would be admitted when the commission's plan became citywide with federal money already committed.

Altogether, more than $1 million was allotted to projects for juveniles during the first two years of the commission's existence—a good investment for the future. To coordinate the work of thirty-four separate agencies in the city, I created a Youth Service Bureau, with the goal of reducing juvenile court cases by 25 percent in five years. Like Rome, a decent regard for the principles of good citizenship was not built in a day. And much as I have been encouraged by the small day-to-day successes in certain areas of the city, like the reduction of serious crime by 31 percent in the areas surrounding hospitals in 1972, it is the long-range programs that will ultimately pay the highest dividends. Half the crimes of violence are committed by juveniles, the sort of crimes that the High Impact Anti-crime Program aims at, and while the high impact guidelines expect "tangible results" within two years, important results are not forecast for five years.

Money for the high impact program was voted by Congress when it found "that the high incidence of crime in the United States threatens the peace, security, and general welfare of the nation. . . ." The funds are administered through the Law Enforcement Assistance Administration. On January 12, 1972, St. Louis was chosen as one of the eight cities in the population class of 500,000 to 1,000,000 to first take part in the program. St. Louis's share: $20 million over five years.

The high impact program is directed at the reduction of "stranger-to-stranger" crimes and burglary. Crimes of violence growing out of family quarrels, or murders among friends and relatives, are apparently considered the result of impetuous or passionate personalities and lack the antisocial nature of street crime. For its investment of $20 million, LEAA expects a decrease in impact crimes of 5 percent in two years and 20 percent in five.

Two weeks after our official designation as an "impact" city, Morris Shenker gave me his resignation as chairman of the St. Louis Commis-

sion on Crime and Law Enforcement. His promised year had stretched
to two, and with the monumental task of preparing a detailed agenda
for implementing the five-year high impact program, he pleaded lack of
time. I accepted his resignation with real regret and appreciation of the
loan of his keen intellect to the city. As Colonel Broston said in adding
his word of thanks, his aid was indispensable to the commission in
becoming an effective coordinating agency.

The high impact program plan, which the commission prepared with
the technical assistance of the Missouri Law Enforcement Assistance
Council Region 5, was delivered to me on April 24, 1972. It is a model
of perceptive analysis of the problems as they exist in St. Louis, as well
as a plan for mobilizing our resources for their solution. It demonstrated what the cooperation between private citizens and their elected
and appointed officials can accomplish.

Reading that program now, and looking back on the first years of
the St. Louis Commission on Crime and Law Enforcement, I find it
hard to believe that during the months our program was getting under
way, a mass-circulation magazine could have actually printed a vicious
personal attack vilifying me and Morris Shenker, calling the commission
a phony and our program a "two-faced fight against crime."

But that's what actually happened.

VII

The Muckrakers and the Crime Commission

Life's Hatchet Job on the Mayor and His Chairman

It is no secret that the picture magazines had for years been trying desperate measures to stem the outflow of good, hard advertising dollars from the print media to the visual medium, television, that doesn't cost anything at the newsstands. The Cowles editors tried to save *Look* with a series of sensational accusations against people in high places, VIPs like the mayor of San Francisco. Mayor Joesph Alioto survived (he was reelected) but *Look* didn't.

Despite *Look's* demise, the big sachems of the Luce tribe decided that muckraking would still pay off if done with the deft, lethal *Life* touch. They would see if scalping a few VIPs in full view of *Life's* 8 million readers wouldn't breathe new life into *Life*. There ensued a series of "investigative reports" that skirted the laws of libel with micrometric closeness. One of the "investigative reports" had been a hatchet job on Governor James A. Rhodes of Ohio. Another victim had been Missouri Senator Edward V. Long, who had been carrying on Tom Hennings' liberal tradition. There is little doubt that *Life's* scalping of Long had cost him the renomination, largely because of *Life's* allegations that the senator had questionable ties with a big-city lawyer who had a successful criminal practice and was Jewish to boot, words calculated to scare the pants off the rural voter.

Although I had been fair game for an unfriendly local press during my twenty-odd years in municipal politics, it had never occurred to me that I too was being trussed up for a coast-to-coast knifing. I didn't really believe it until May 18, 1970, when I got an indication that something was in the wind. I was playing squash at the Missouri Athletic Club when a boy brought word that there was a phone call for me.

"Take his number and tell him I'll call back when we've finished the game," I told the lad.

"The party says it's urgent, sir."

So I went down from the squash courts to the fifth floor and picked up the phone. It was Allen Molasky, president of Pierce News Co., the major magazine distributor for the St. Louis area. He asked: "Al, do you know that *Life* Magazine is doing a story on you?"

"A state senator called me from Jefferson City a few months ago," I said, "to tell me some *Life* people had been nosing around the capital. But it must be just a rumor, Allen. What is there to write about? Besides, they'd certainly come to see me first."

"I don't think it's a rumor," he persisted. "The *Life* people called me to say I'd better order extra copies because the issue was going to be a hot seller. They're calling the story 'The Mayor, the Mob, and the Mouthpiece.' "

I still found it hard to believe, but I thanked him and asked him to check his sources and make absolutely sure.

When I got back to the office I had Bob Duffe do a little checking on his own. Then I called Allen Molasky again. He had checked, and sure enough, the story was not a rumor. He knew the name of the man *Life* was calling "the Mouthpiece": Morris Shenker, of course.

On my way home to dinner that evening I recalled Morris Shenker's warning when I offered him the chairmanship of the Commission on Crime and Law Enforcement: "You'd better think it over. . . ." Well, I had thought it over, I had appointed him, and I had no regrets, whatever *Life* chose to say about him—or me.

I could now pinpoint the author of the *Life* story and guess pretty accurately what he was going to say. The writer was certainly Denny Walsh, a local crime reporter who had tried unsuccessfully to sell a bit of fiction about Mayor Cervantes to the *Globe-Democrat,* and when it was turned down he took off for the big leagues where he would be appreciated. At least *Life* had hired him. Denny Walsh had been in and out of City Hall for some time, and I must admit that over the years our acquaintance had not ripened into close friendship. We didn't see eye-to-eye on a number of issues. And since 1969, when he shared a Pulitzer prize with *Globe-Democrat* reporter Al Delugach, his hats had become several sizes too small. He was confident that he knew more about crime from both sides of the law than the late Al Capone and J. Edgar Hoover combined ever knew. And if Denny Walsh had succeeded in pawning off his malignant fairy tales on *Life* as gospel truth, I was in for a bad time, not only politically but personally. My family and friends—all St. Louis in fact—were going to be hurt.

As soon as I got home, I called Carmen aside and told her that we could expect an unpleasant surprise in the next issue of *Life* but I could give her no details.

"We'd better get the boys ready for it," Carmen said.

That remark was characteristic of Carmen. With her woman's sensitivity she foresaw what lay ahead for all of us, and she was going to make sure from the beginning that the burden wouldn't fall on my shoulders alone. She suggested that it probably wouldn't be as bad as I anticipated.

"They're going to say I'm buddy-buddy with some of our most accomplished hoodlums," I said, "and *Life* isn't an insignificant butcher-paper magazine that nobody reads. The story is going to make a big noise and the kids are going to suffer. They're going to take a lot of guff from unfeeling classmates. I can hear the little darlings now: 'So your old man's a gangster! Why doesn't he make you wear a gun?' I think we should prepare them for it right away."

But we decided to wait a day or two. If I could get hold of an advance copy I would know more specifically what I was talking about.

My staff tried to break through the secrecy barrier that *Life* had built around the "investigative report." Dave Meeker, whom I had hired away from the *Post-Dispatch,* called to *Life* in New York but learned nothing about what the article contained.

I wired Ralph Graves, *Life* managing editor, demanding the elementary courtesy of being confronted with any article concerning me before publication. I understood that Governor Rhodes and Senator

Long had at least been accorded that privilege before *Life* threw them to the wolves. But Graves played dead.

When I learned that the magazine was being printed at the Reuben H. Donnelly plant in Chicago, I phoned my friend Mayor Richard Daley in the Windy City. If anybody in Chicago could get his hands on an advance copy it would be Dick Daley. I couldn't reach him during the day but he returned my call at home that night.

"Don't worry what those damned Eastern interests are up to, Al," said Daley. "They're just trying to sell magazines."

It was all old hat to Dick, who had been a whipping boy so often that he had grown callouses. For me, I told him, it was a new and disagreeable experience.

"I'll try to get a copy for you," Daley said. "Meanwhile take it easy."

Even His Honor couldn't get an advance copy.

Next day Dave Meeker learned that Al Delugach, who had worked with Walsh on the *Globe* but had gone over to the *Post-Dispatch,* had left for New York where he had had a privileged look at his ex-teammate's story. So Delugach was able to file a story for the Sunday *Post-Dispatch* the day before the on-sale date of *Life,* thus enabling the *Post* to scoop Walsh's old paper. Evidently Walsh still harbored a grudge against the *Globe* for not printing his fiction about the mayor.

When Delugach called me for comment, he had to give me an inkling of what Walsh's story was about so that I could give him a statement, the gist of which was: "The preposterous allegations contained in the upcoming issue of *Life* concerning myself and my administration would warrant no comment if they did not have such tragic implications on my personal reputation and that of the community."

I added that if *Life* published the slurs he had repeated to me it would show an irresponsible disregard for the truth. After promising a point-by-point reply when I had read the article, I concluded: "*Life* magazine's use of innuendo, guilt by association, subtle but false inferences and simple error in fact will be dealt with in the public arena where the people of St. Louis can see the truth first-hand and make their judgments accordingly. I am confident that they will not accept irresponsible journalism any more than they will accept irresponsible government."

Half a dozen more efforts to reach Graves in New York were

ignored, as were two telegrams I sent off to Time, Inc., publishers of *Life*. We did get a promise from the promotion department to deliver a copy of the pestiferous issue to City Hall on Sunday noon, the day before publication. But I actually saw a copy—from a distance—several hours before Sunday noon.

I was walking home from the cathedral after mass when John Auble, a television newscaster, jumped from the KSD-TV station wagon that pulled up to the curb.

"Any comment on this story, Mr. Mayor?" he asked. The cameras zeroed in on us as he waved a copy of *Life* at me.

"Not until I've read it," I replied. "You're way ahead of me." Somebody had obviously broken the release date and given the media the jump on us.

We had set up a strategy meeting that afternoon at the Chase Hotel. The principal victims of Denny Walsh's character assassination were there: Morris Shenker, of course; Jack Murphy, my attorney; and Tony Sansone, who was also one of my most active political supporters. There was my staff—the old war-horse Bob Duffe, a one-time veteran of the *Globe-Democrat* who had capably served my predecessor Mayor Raymond Tucker and whom I had asked to continue on as my executive secretary, Dave Meeker, a former City Hall reporter for the *Post-Dispatch*; and my newest staffer, Ed Ruesing, who had recently come over from the City Art Museum, where he had been public relations officer. Sitting in at my request was attorney Mortimer A. Rosecan, an expert on libel law.

The magazine's makeup editor helped set the stage for the editorial lynching, first with the yellow promotional sticker on the cover: "PHONY CRIME FIGHT IN ST. LOUIS," and then on the inside with a two-page spread with dignified photos in living color of Mayor Cervantes and his crime commissioner, white-haired Morris Shenker. The caption, in capitals, announced, "A TWO-FACED CRIME FIGHT IN ST. LOUIS." Slightly less alarming type said, "Both the mayor and his crime commissioner have personal ties to the underworld."

A picture in the article showed me at a microphone with Tony Sansone—at a Christmas-tree lighting ceremony—not a very sinister occasion, really, but the scare caption here read: "The man closest to the Mayor is the confidant—and son-in-law of a Mob boss."

Next we had a series of six photos stepping down diagonally across two pages showing a youthful black-haired Shenker progressively graying and wearing glasses as he was pictured representing a rogues' gallery of some of Missouri's ablest malefactors, from gambler Sid Wyman to Teamster boss Jimmy Hoffa. Mayor Cervantes was nowhere to be seen until the next page. Here he was shown receiving an award for "a 1969 fact-finding trip to Israel while Morris Shenker looked on"—possibly a grandstand play for the Jewish vote, but hardly a Mafia operation.

My blood pressure rose as I read the text which was in part slyly damning by implication, in part outright falsehood, and the rest a rehash of tired old complaints which my opponents exhumed every time I ran for office, but which apparently did not impress the electorate.

I was particularly infuriated by the slur on the city of St. Louis and the insult to our crime commission. Walsh spoke of a federal task force being sent to St. Louis to "do battle with organized crime" that "some public officials treat with hypocrisy." Actually the task force was headquartered in St. Louis to deal with organized crime in the states of Missouri, Kansas and Southern Illinois, just as twelve other cities are headquarters for similar task forces with multistate jurisdiction. Walsh also wrote that "the President's Crime Commission" said in 1967 that organized crime "flourished in St. Louis." In fact the President's Crime Commission on Law Enforcement and Justice in 1967 didn't even mention St. Louis in the chapter devoted to organized crime.

Actually organized crime has withered to a sorry shadow of what it was in St. Louis in the 1940s and early 1950s. The police, under Colonel Broston and his successor Eugene J. Camp, have pretty well cleaned out syndicate-controlled crime. What prostitution survives is strictly private enterprise and local talent. The big-shot gamblers who used to operate from across the Mississippi in East St. Louis, Illinois, have largely moved to the Far West. The narcotics traffic is, by its nature, supplied from outside sources, but addiction in St. Louis was no greater than in other cities of equal size, and our program of narcotics control and rehabilitation, amply bolstered by federal funds, was moving smoothly ahead.

The phrase "phony crime fight" was an outrageous slander. I had campaigned personally day and night to persuade the city to vote a sales tax and two bond issues aimed directly at controlling crime. And the taxpayers voted "yes" by majorities ranging from 68 to better than 78 percent.

As for the crime commission itself, it was never intended to take over the police function. It was designed, like other subsystems of the Challenge of the Seventies program, to involve interested citizens in community problems, to coordinate related agencies, to seek out flaws in present law enforcement and criminal justice practices, and to make recommendations for their improvement.*

As for Morris Shenker, he was one of my finest appointments. I had known him for years but that did not prevent him from supporting my opponents in the two most important races of my political life—when I ran against Donald Gunn for president of the board of aldermen in 1963 and lost, and when I defeated incumbent Mayor Tucker a few years later. I respected Shenker's legal talents, his business acumen, and his fund-raising ability for both Jewish and Christian charities.

A successful criminal lawyer does not build his practice or gain national reputation by defending Mothers Superior, astrophysicists or Thomist philosophers. The nature of his calling had brought Shenker into contact with newsworthy transgressors, and the juxtaposition of names in the press had over the years given him a veneer of guilt by association.

---

*The roster of the original citizen members of the St. Louis Commission on Crime and Law Enforcement gives an idea of the caliber and expertise of the dedicated men and women who served: Narcotics: Nobel Don Mitchell, an ex-addict, founder and director of the Narcotics Service Council. Schools: Dr. H. G. Mellman, Political Science Department, University of Missouri–St. Louis. Juvenile Delinquency: Dr. Fredda Witherspoon, Board of Children's Welfare Services and professor at Forest Park Junior College. Courts: R. D. Fitzgibbon, former U.S. attorney, Eastern District, Missouri. Legislative: David M. Grant, attorney, research director, board of aldermen. Police: Thomas Carroll, chairman Fifth District Police Community Council, Council on Human Relations member. Research: Dr. Gordon Misner, director of Research, University of Missouri-St. Louis. Community Involvement: Harry Fender, former police officer, KMOX radio producer. Auto Theft: Thomas P. Cox, Jr., public affairs manager, Allstate Insurance.

The press had also gleefully gone after him for his alignment in the late forties with a local faction of the Democratic party known to editorial writers as the Shenker-Callanan machine. The Steamfitters were and still are among the whipping boys of the St. Louis newspapers and Callanan was influential in the Steamfitters' Union.

The press was often happily apt to overlook the fact that Shenker's interest in crime was not restricted to the moneyed finagler who could afford his fees. He was deeply concerned with the rehabilitation of the penniless convict after he got out of jail and was trying to readjust to society. He had given his time, money and effort to the work of Father Dismas Clark, my freshman English teacher. Father Clark, who took the name of the thief asking forgiveness of Christ while hanging on the cross beside Him, founded Dismas House, a halfway refuge for newly released convicts—with Morris Shenker's help. In fact, *Life's* photo of Shenker standing with Jimmy Hoffa was taken at the premiere of *The Hoodlum Priest,* a film based on the work of Father Clark.

While the air in the Chase Hotel turned blue with the indignant comments of my fellow victims, I went through the list of bad guys pictured in *Life's* double-truck gallery—hooligans who were supposed to be my links with the underworld, I read them aloud, one by one:

—Jimmy Carroll, dubbed "the betting commissioner" by St. Louis sports writers because his odds on any sporting event in the country were quoted as "official." He was photographed with Shenker at the Kefauver hearings in the 1950s. Jimmy hadn't been quoting odds while I was in City Hall. He died in California some years ago.

—Sidney Wyman, also snapped during the Kefauver probe. Wyman was supposed to be a really big-time gambler. Long before I became mayor, however, he had moved all his operations to Las Vegas where, people tell me, gambling is legal.

—John Vitale (1952) is a sharp-nosed St. Louis hood, a legendary figure who I understand is being watched so closely by the cops that he complains regularly to John Doherty, chief of St. Louis police detectives, that his civil rights are being violated. I have never met Vitale.

—Buster Wortman was next of the historic characters, reputed to be a boss racketeer on the Illinois side of the Mississippi. I have never seen Wortman, but he could scarcely be a factor in my "phony fight against crime." Wortman, too, was long dead before *Life's* charade reached the newsstands.

—"Mafia client Shorty Caleca" was *Life's* identification of the man outside the courtroom in 1958 with his coat over his head. Even without the coat I would not have recognized him. I have never seen Caleca.

As for Jimmy Hoffa—and here I must at least give *Life* good marks for crediting Morris Shenker with being co-founder with the Hoodlum Priest of Dismas House—while I was getting used to my new office in the City Hall, Hoffa was getting settled in his cell at the federal penitentiary, Lewisburg, Pennsylvania. Even the brilliant Shenker could not save him. It took no less a person that the president of the United States to spring Jimmy the Christmas before the 1972 election.

I turned back to the preceding page where there was a small 1959 shot of Jimmy Michaels, described there as "boss of the Syrian Mob." The attempt here was to tie me to Michaels through my friend and former business associate, Tony Sansone.

I first met Mr. Michaels in 1954 at Tony's wedding. I saw him as the genial, good-looking father of the bride. Mr. Michaels' name had been associated with the rough-and-tumble activities of the Roaring Twenties, but his activities as a youth had no relevance to Tony or me.

When Mary Anne's mother died, I of course went to the funeral. At neither of our meetings did Michaels and I exchange more than a few polite but unpolitical words. Yet, here is more of Walsh's fiction:

> In December, 1964, just two days after Cervantes declared his candidacy for the Mayor, he met with Sansone and Michaels to plan campaign strategy. The meeting took place in the office of the Rite-Way Cigarette Sales, a gang-controlled vending machine firm. . . .

The alleged meeting, of course, never took place. But Walsh had even taller stories in his typewriter:

> The following March, after Cervantes had won the primary, Sansone again met with Michaels at Rite-Way to talk over Cervantes' prospects for the general election. This time, Giordano, the Mafia boss, sat in too.

That alleged meeting also did not take place. Walsh invented other fictional ties between the mayor and Michaels, such as the allegation that Michaels brokered insurance through my insurance firm until 1952.

It was documented by the insurance commissioner of the state of Missouri that Mr. Michaels had never brokered insurance with our company before or after 1952.

The height of Walsh's imaginative writing was in a paragraph alleging that following Mrs. Michaels' funeral I had helped tend bar at a gathering of what Walsh termed "the royalty of organized crime in St. Louis." I did not attend such a gathering—I was not even aware that there had been one.

This was a matter on which I had already confronted Walsh. He had called me on the phone to start a conversation that I learned later was being tape-recorded without my knowledge. He'd be a great candidate for the Nixon administration. I can still hear the slow monotone of Walsh's voice as he asked me if it was true that I had attended a get-together after the funeral. The question seemed ridiculous at the time and I dismissed it out of hand—"curtly," as Walsh claimed when debating the matter with Duncan Bauman, publisher of the *Globe-Democrat;* and Walsh played back the tape to Bauman to prove I was curt.

Bauman didn't need the tape. Of course I was curt. Walsh approached everything happening at City Hall with such built-in contempt that I sometimes found it difficult to offer him more than minimal courtesy. Drunk or sober, Walsh always had a chip on his shoulder and was never happier than when he thought he had an axe handle to beat me with. It was not difficult to be curt in saying "hell no" to a man who insinuates that you favor organized crime in your city. The *Globe* never did run the story. Walsh had to wait for *Life* to publish the libel.

Despite my categorical denial of having attended that "gathering," Walsh was determined to get his story into the *Globe.* Soon after our conversation, I had a phone call tipping me off that the story was already in type.

I immediately called publisher Dunc Bauman, asking him to hold up the story until he could check its accuracy. Then if he found it to be true, he had my full blessing to go ahead and print it.

To suggest sources who could confirm my denial, I read Bauman my calendar for the day, June 9, 1967. That busy day did indeed start with my going to a funeral mass in South St. Louis for Mrs. James Michaels, at the Church of the Immaculate Conception. After mass, my schedule was so full that I couldn't get to the graveside at Calvary Cemetery in North St. Louis. Instead I went directly from the church to City Hall to meet Joseph Griesedieck, president of Falstaff Brewing Corporation and a trustee for the National Council for Crime and Delinquency.

At 11:30 a.m., I was signing a proclamation for the American Radiology Technicians represented by Leslie Wilson of the University of Missouri Medical Center, Sister Aloysius Marie Borst of St. Louis University, and Mrs. Jobeth Worden, American Society of Radiologists, Port Arthur, Texas. Dunc Bauman agreed that they seemed reasonably respectable.

Fifteen minutes later I had signed another proclamation from the Painters and Decorators Association. Among that delegation was Richard L. Sullivan of the *Globe Democrat.*

I hadn't gone out for lunch. That day I was host to a catered lunch in my office for twenty-odd members of the board of aldermen, which lasted until well past two o'clock.

I listed my afternoon appointments up to the time of going home for a quick bite of dinner. Then Carmen and I dressed for the seven o'clock wedding of Patricia Ann Salvadore to Michael Patrick Duffy at St. Louis Cathedral. The bride was the daughter of the Cathedral organist. The reception across the street lasted until 11 p.m.

I had given Bauman the names of at least a hundred people who could tell him that I was not pouring booze that day. He was convinced. The Walsh story was killed as far as the *Globe-Democrat* was concerned.

I had gone to mass twice on that crowded June 9, 1967, but apparently I had not prayed hard enough.

Shortly thereafter Walsh had left the *Globe* and St. Louis in a huff, carting off many cartons of documents from the *Globe* files, the tapes of our phone conversation, and, I understand, the *Globe's* tape recorder. He headed for New York and *Life* where he showed himself to be a man of miracles. He resurrected the corpse of the story the *Globe-Democrat* had killed.

II

There were other maddening things in the *Life* story. The mud thrown at me and Morris Shenker had bespattered not only Tony Sansone but some of my other friends by implication. Attorney Jack Murphy, for instance, had been a special agent for the FBI for four years, and the late J. Edgar Hoover did not usually train his men to be mobsters. To Walsh, however, he was a shady character.

Or Jerry Bollato, accused by Walsh of tricky dealings, who had served with the U.S. military government team in Japan, with the Air Force intelligence in the Korean War, and in Alaska on a top-secret project. He was recalled to the service during the Berlin crisis, served as staff judge advocate at the Toul-Rosiers air force base in France and at the time of the Walsh mudslinging caper was a lieutenant colonel in the Air National Guard with top-security clearance. He was in charge of security and law enforcement for the fighter wing.

To see men pilloried because they happened to be friends of mine gave me an acute attack of nausea.

There was also a lot of warmed-over oatmeal in Walsh's article, allegations of favoritism at City Hall, a retelling of the sale of my interest in Consolidated Service Car to Tony Sansone, and his subsequent sale of the fleet to the local transit company. All these charges had been aired every time I ran for high office, but in the final analysis, the "scandals" all turned out to be legal and ethical transactions.

Well, the *Life* promotion department had done an excellent job of plastering the country with a release timed to make the morning papers, which meant that the locals would have the story in their early editions that very night, March 24. We victims gathered at the Chase Hotel had to be ready with ammunition for the counterattack.

We agreed that the first step was to demand an objective investigation of *Life's* charges by an impartial agency, and a three-pronged approach was voted. The most logical and trustworthy investigative body we could think of was mentioned in the first paragraph of Walsh's article: the Federal Strike Force which Walsh said had been sent "to do battle with organized crime in the City of St. Louis." So we drafted a letter to William D. Jones, attorney in charge of the Task Force on

Organized Crime and Racketeering in St. Louis, requesting a probe into the charges.

Next we decided to send a similar letter to the local arm of the Justice Department—federal District Attorney Daniel Bartlett, Jr. After all, if the substance of the Walsh-*Life* charges were true, District Attorney Bartlett was open to charges of laxity and would of course want to get the facts as quickly as possible.

Finally, there was the local police department, which to my mind was as intelligent and tough-minded about organized crime as any in the country and had done a bang-up job of keeping the families in the area pretty much subdued. Furthermore the St. Louis police force was, by a curious quirk of history, carefully insulated from local political influence and thus well equipped for an impartial investigation.

Two weeks before the outbreak of the Civil War in 1861, the then governor of Missouri, one Claiborne F. Jackson, got the state legislature to pass a law giving the state control of the St. Louis Police Department, with a board of police commissioners appointed by the governor. St. Louis was a center of pro-Union feeling, while much of the rest of the state was in sympathy with the Confederacy. The governor had every intention of using the St. Louis police as an arm of the Confederate Army. In July of 1861, Jackson was deposed as governor and fled south with his followers to join the Confederacy. But more than a century later, the St. Louis police are still controlled from Jefferson City.

The Commissioner of Police at the time of the *Life* crisis was Col. James Sanders, who could hardly be called an intimate of mine, since I understand he was for my opponent when I first ran for mayor. He was, however, a man of unquestioned integrity. We drafted a letter to him, too, seeking an impartial inquiry.

Our paper work, including the text of my statement for the seven o'clock press conference, was finished with only ten minutes to spare. Although the content was much the same as my statement to Delugach, I was afraid I would not be able to keep the angry indignation out of my voice. I did manage to make my points without a quaver as I read to the assembled reporters: "I was amazed, outraged and angered by the preposterous lies . . . a sinister, calculated smear designed to boost circulation and advertising at my expense and the expense of my family and our city. . . . I will fight this magazine's flagrant irresponsibility in the public arena before the people of St. Louis. . . ."

I would have more to say at my regular Monday morning press conference. I would call for the three-pronged investigation we had mapped, and I would announce the filing of a $12 million libel suit against Time, Inc., publishers of *Life,* and Danny Walsh—$2 million for substantive damages and $10 million punitive.

III

At home that night I sat on the sofa and sought calm in a scotch on the rocks as I went over the day's events with Carmen. I also tried to assess the real damage that would accrue when *Life* hit the streets next morning. Although it was hard to estimate the intangibles, $12 million did seem to be an underestimate.

The attack on my integrity cut deep, and the wounds would be slow-healing. The injury to my political career was critical. Any hopes I had for seeking the governorship of Missouri—and I admit they were quite high in view of important backing—had been cynically shot down. While I was confident that many St. Louisans knew me well enough to take the slander with a liberal shakerful of salt, to many more, particularly the nonurban voters who are always ready to believe the worst of any city dweller, the printed word is next to gospel.

My family, too, had been badly hurt. Luckily my dress-rehearsal with the boys a few nights earlier had been successful. Our oldest son, A.J., was working on a special project at Webster College and carrying on several successful business ventures on the side. When I heard his reaction—"It's just another outrage on the public by one branch of the corrupt Establishment"—I knew that he would weather the storm.

I was afraid the younger ones might be more vulnerable. They were all at good Catholic schools: Craig at Christian Brothers, Barry at St. Louis University High, and Brett at Chaminade. I told them they might expect some of their schoolmates to swallow whole the slimy things the magazine would print, and that they might say thoughtless and ugly things, even though the article was a series of innuendos and untruths.

Barry spoke for the four of them when he said: "But we know *you* Dad, so we know things like that couldn't be true."

I was proud of them for their faith in me. We had thought of keeping them out of school for a few days, but now I was convinced they had all the courage they needed to face the taunts they were sure to hear.

Carmen had always had more than enough courage for two, and she had it now, even though she was badly hurt. I could see how badly when the phone rang.

It was our married daughter Judy calling from her home in the Houston suburbs. The early newscasts of Texas TV stations had already picked up the *Life* release, and she was beginning to hear derisive laughter over the phone. "Well, well! So your old man travels with the mob! Ha-ha!" She was crying when she hung up.

That afternoon I had read in Tony Sansone's face the price he was paying for being my friend. And as Carmen told me of her conversation with Judy, I learned what it cost to be my wife and daughter.

IV

By next morning the damage done to the image of the City of St. Louis became apparent. The nation's headline writers were having a picnic with *Life's* wicked press release, gaily destroying the city's pride in itself which I had been laboring for more than four years to build.

"MAYOR OF ST. LOUIS LINKED TO MAFIA," screamed the *Riverside* (Calif.) *Daily Enterprise* without attribution. The *Dayton* (Ohio) *Daily News* was more circumspect: "LIFE CLAIMS MAYOR, MOB LINKED." Not the *Kansas City Star,* however: "LINK CERVANTES TO CRIME KINGS." The understatement of the year came when *Chicago Today* picked up my press conference statement as well as the *Life* release: "ST. LOUIS MAYOR MIFFED." Miffed indeed!

Simultaneous with the announcement of my libel suit I fired off telegrams ($29.10 worth) to the president of Time, Inc., and to managing editor Graves of *Life,* demanding five pages in the next issue of *Life* "to repudiate the totally false allegations toward myself and the City of St. Louis."

Graves' reply was addressed to "The Honorable Alfonso J.

Cervantes." Doesn't he believe what he reads in his own magazine? Graves offered me a "response of suitable length in our regular forum, the Letters Page. However, Life reserves the right to decide how much space to give any such letter as well as the issue in which the reply will appear. . . ."

Space for a letter to the editor in answer to eight pages of libelous trash seemed to me to be as unfair and unjust as the original article, and I told Graves so in rejecting his offer as completely unacceptable.

I was greatly encouraged, though, by the attitude of the local press, including papers not usually friendly to Cervantes. The day after *Life* appeared, Walsh's old paper, the *St. Louis Globe-Democrat,* printed an editorial under the title "Guilty by Sketchy Association" that said in part:

> Most of the substantive facts cited by Writer Denny Walsh in the current issue of Life magazine had some time ago been published in the Globe-Democrat. But we did not and would not state on the basis of our own extended investigation that Mayor Alfonso J. Cervantes has "business and personal ties with gangsters that operate in this city," as Life does. Had this newspaper been convinced, having virtually all the facts contained in the Life story, of any Cervantes connection with crime in St. Louis we would have published it at the time. And if any proof can be developed in the future, we will print it.

A few days later the *Post-Dispatch* came to bat for our side. *Post* editorial writers had always regarded me with a cold and fishy eye, but they had always been scrupulously fair, as they were in this case. Unless *Life* can produce more documentation, said the *Post* editorially, "than has so far been shown through its innuendos, hints of guilt by association and statements essentially irrelevant to the central accusation, the Mayor has been wronged and so has the City of St. Louis." The editorial continued:

> Everybody in St. Louis knows by now that Mr. Cervantes, with whom we have had our differences, is an optimistic and flamboyant promoter who as alderman exhibited somewhat less than

the most-finely-tuned appreciation of what conflict of interest is, but who performed well enough as mayor to earn a second term. To say this is far from hinting that he is a sinister figure enmeshed in the machinations of an underworld "ethnic mob". .·. . The visible evidence does not support the correlative accusation of *Life* that "organized crime flourishes here." On the contrary, the city seems to be free of the symptoms of such crime. On this point and on the Mayor's probity *Life* . . . has not convinced us.

The electronic media also refuted *Life's* charges. The CBS outlet, KMOX, objected to the magazine's "dubious journalistic technique." Other radio stations came to similar conclusions and all deplored the undeserved low blow at St. Louis.

If I had worried what my former neighbors in South St. Louis would say when the good hausfraus discussed the article over the back fences behind their neat little bungalows, I could set my mind at rest after reading the front-page editorial in the *South Side Journal.* Editor-publisher of the *Journal* was Frank Bick, who kept a close watch on City Hall and never failed to let me know by phone or by editorial when he didn't like what was going on. Bick wrote:

In an article written by a simple-minded former St. Louis reporter named Denny Walsh Life took a collection of lies, half truths, and misleading outlines and tore asunder the reputation of A. J. Cervantes. . . .

The Post has never had any love for Cervantes and has always made it a practice to publish anything at all which put him in a bad light. Yet in their wildest diatribes they never attempted a smear like the one Life has vomited up. . . .

We wish the Mayor well in his libel suit but we are afraid he is wasting his time. Recent Supreme Court rulings have made it virtually impossible for anyone in public life to win a libel suit. We think most people will see the article for what it is and forget about it. . . .

The *South St. Louis Neighborhood News* chimed in a few weeks later and added the satisfying results of our appeal to competent

authorities to confirm or deny the accusation that the city was wide
open to the Mafia:

> The President of the Board of Police Commissioners, James
> Sanders, has stated that organized crime does not flourish in St.
> Louis. The present police chief Eugene J. Camp and his prede-
> cessor Curtis Brostron have both stated publicly that organized
> crime does not flourish in St. Louis. Aloys P. Kaufmann, former
> mayor and president of the Chamber of Commerce and a Repub-
> lican stated that organized crime does not flourish in St. Louis.
> Mr. Kaufman has voted against Mayor Cervantes in the last two
> elections so his voice should not be prejudiced. This is fairly
> conclusive proof to us. . . .

The labor press and the black periodicals were also on my side. The
Labor Tribune gleefully took Denny Walsh apart for his past journalistic performances:

> We know that Walsh, as crime reporter for the conservative St.
> Louis Globe-Democrat, and a colleague did write a series of
> articles on crime in St. Louis—much of it warned over, transmog-
> rified stuff which Ted Wagner of the liberal Post-Dispatch had
> "interpretively" written 15 or 20 years back. And to our
> amazement they shared a Pulitzer prize for it.

The Argus, a black paper which had been violent about one of the
past transactions dug up in the *Life* article, declared: "The dead file is
the proper place for the matter to remain." Another black periodical,
The Crusader, saw the whole business as an attempt by Walsh "to bury
the mayor politically."

Nothing the press had to say, however, was as reassuring as a
long-distance call I received from the man who was—and still is—closer
to me than any one of my friends and counsellors. And this man is not,
as *Life* declared, Tony Sansone; he is my brother Lu—Father Lucius F.
Cervantes, S.J., Ph.D. Lu was the architect of "The Challenge of the
Seventies," which included among its subsystems the Commission on
Crime and Law Enforcement. When the *Life* article appeared Lu was in

Washington setting up an office in the capital for our Challenge program and getting FBI approval for our Crime Commission. I have always admired Lu. I respect him and listen to his wise counsel. He, in turn, is loyal to me, but his primary committment is to his Jesuit vows. If he were ever forced to choose between his loyalty to me and his devotion to God and clean government, I know where I would end up. Had I actually been involved with hoods and gangsters (and Lu has been around me enough to know what's going on) he would have been obliged to make that choice.

That's why Lu's expression of confidence during those dismal days meant so much to me.

V

Despite editor-publisher Frank Bick's gloomy prediction that I would be wasting my time with a libel suit, I was determined to get legal satisfaction from Time, Inc., and Denny Walsh. Morty Rosecan, whom I had retained on the advice of my personal attorney, Jack Murphy, with the concurrence of Duncan Bauman of the *Globe-Democrat* (no stranger to libel suits), though we had a chance. I was aware of the Supreme Court ruling that a public figure, in order to win a verdict in a libel case, must prove that the writer had demonstrated "malice," but it was clear to me that Denny Walsh was not motivated by a love of St. Louis and civic virtue, when, in the face of all evidence to the contrary, he carried his fictional garbage (which his own former boss had rejected) to a wider and less perceptive market. Apparently it was clear to Morty Rosecan, too, because he filed for a hearing before the U.S. District Court for the Eastern District of Missouri.

Morty's willingness to fight for me was not without the realization that the cards were stacked pretty much against a politician in a libel suit. In deciding the *New York Times* case in 1964, the Supreme Court ruled that a public official cannot recover damages unless he can prove "actual malice." Furthermore, he must demonstrate by a "convincing clarity of the proofs" that a news story was written "with knowledge that it was false, or with a reckless disregard for whether it was false or not." This is a far cry from the day when a man suing for libel merely had to read the defamatory publication in court. It was then up to the defendant to prove the truth of his charges. Since 1964, the burden of proof is apparently up to the official.

We went into court with the subpoenaed tapes of Walsh's conversations with me and with Sansone, on which we both denied the bartending-for-hoods incident. We produced a copy of the report by Sgt. Ed Schaaf of the St. Louis Police Intelligence Unit recording his own version of the March 1965 meeting described by Walsh. Sgt. Schaaf made no mention of Cervantes or of any political plotting.

The court however found for the defendant. Some of my friends deplored the fact that Judge James A. Meredith was a friend of mine and had therefore bent over backwards to establish his impartiality. Personally, I am convinced that he was merely hewing to the line drawn by the Supreme Court.

It was clear that this was the basis for the action by the U.S. Court of Appeals for the Eighth Circuit when it rejected my appeal, declaring that:

> long standing decisions of the Supreme Court make clear that the mayor is obligated to demonstrate with convincing clarity that the materials he alleges to be defamatory were published with knowledge of their falsity or with reckless disregard for the truth. Whereas here the published materials objectively considered in the light of all the evidence must be taken as having been published in good faith without actual malice and on the basis of careful verification efforts. . . .

The "good faith" and "careful verification efforts" accepted by the appeals court seem to have been based largely on a report by an anonymous Department of Justice agent (who I am sure is a mythical figure invented by Walsh) who had leaked the contents of a confidential paper to Walsh. The verification efforts by *Life* researchers did not extend as far as a courtesy interview with me prior to publication. Walsh refused to identify his (so-called) secret sources and the appeals court declined to require him to do so. Although it did not hold that reporters enjoy a constitutional right to protect news sources, the court found they deserved some protection.

The appeal was dismissed.

There remained an appeal to the U.S. Supreme Court, which has allowed reporters to go to jail for refusing to divulge news sources—but not in libel cases involving public officials who did not demonstrate malice with convincing clarity.

On January 15, 1973, the U.S. Supreme Court, stubbornly adhering to its 1964 guidelines, declined to review the appellate court's dismissal of my case.

There must be some mysterious agency governing the fate of men and magazines, some instrument of poetic justice higher than our highest court. Two weeks before the Supreme Court's decision, *Life* magazine, its last-gasp venture into muckraking an economic failure, published its final issue.

The last I heard, investigative reporter Denny Walsh had managed to peddle a leftover hatchet job on a U.S. senator to the good, gray *New York Times,* and was functioning as innuendo-and-guilt-by-association specialist for that august daily.

VIII

Teach a Man to Fish

Businessmen Join Fight
Against Prejudice and Unemployment

The whole city seemed to be up in arms. I had been mayor for less than a year and angry citizens were already talking about a recall petition. Little children were spitting at me in the street. Editorial writers accused me of wanting to destroy the school system and return St. Louis to the Dark Ages. City Hall was invaded daily by protesting groups of teachers, parents and pupils—black, white, and integrated. A stranger might have believed that I must have been guilty of at least child molesting or selling black children into slavery.

Actually, all I had done was to ask experts to study a request by the school board for a 28-cent tax boost before giving it my blessing.

In truth the school board did not need my blessing. The St. Louis Board of Education is an independent political entity. Its members are individually elected and it has its own taxing power. However, the board was convinced that my endorsement was essential before going to the voters. The same request for a tax increase to a $2.51 rate had been defeated at a previous election (at which only 20 percent of the electorate voted) and the board was understandably anxious to avoid another failure.

There is no doubt that most great cities tend to have education systems that are somewhat less than great. Equally true is the fact that most big cities are bankrupt. There is an obvious connection between the two facts. As I was elected on a promise to make the city live within its means if at all possible, I have always been budget-minded, and it was second nature for me to question the board's balance sheet. I was already bothered by the $200,000 the two elections were costing the city, and I was determined to make sure that the board of education was running an efficient operation before I endorsed the tax request. I did not consider myself enough of an expert on school administration to trust my own judgment. I therefore asked the U.S. Commissioner of Education, the Ford Foundation and the Danforth Foundation to agree on a panel of four to evaluate the St. Louis school budget.

The blue-ribbon panel consisted of Merrimon Cuninggim, executive director of the Danforth Foundation, Delmar Cobble, assistant commissioner of education for the state of Missouri, Forrest W. Harrison, finance specialist for the U.S. Office of Education, and John Polley, specialist in educational finance for the Columbia University Teachers College. The experts met to review the St. Louis budget while the media and the educators continued their guerrilla warfare on Mayor Cervantes, the enemy of learning.

The school board mustered endorsements from Episcopal Bishop George Cadigan, head of the Metropolitan Church Federation; from Cardinal Ritter, who issued a pastoral letter soliciting votes; from the St. Louis Labor Council; the president of the Chamber of Commerce; and Local 197 of the American Federation of Musicians. Delegations continued to storm City Hall, and Herbert Rothenberg, president of the Public School Patrons Alliance, went ahead with his recall petition which he was going to circulate if the mayor withheld his approval and the tax measure lost.

Meanwhile, my blue-ribbon panel reported that the school budget was not only water-tight, but that the tax increase was probably too little to meet the system's needs. I immediately issued my endorsement.

And I was immediately attacked by the newspapers for taking so long to make a decision which, they said, was not only reluctant but confusing to the voters.

The voters were not confused, but I was. It has taken me years to learn that no matter what decision I make, there were bound to be squawks of rage and outrage from somewhere along the banks of the Mississippi.

Money, or rather the lack of it, has been the bane of the public school system in St. Louis as in all big cities, with their dwindling tax bases seeping away to the suburbs. We are worse off than many cities because we get insufficient financial help from the state of Missouri and because St. Louis County, where too many of our most affluent taxpayers have moved, has its own school system. Suburban schools spend twice as much to educate a child as the city does. For instance Clayton, a community of 16,000 just across the St. Louis city line, spends $1,600 a year for each pupil. St. Louis city spends only $800.

Most of the city's expense goes for teachers' salaries, which, while not munificent, are well above the penury level. The city teacher's average pay at the beginning of the seventies was a little more than $10,000 a year, perhaps a little lower than the national median. Beginning teachers got $7,200, earning up to $12,600, top. If the money were available, we would have had more teachers per pupil. Classes were too big to allow for individual attention, averaging thirty-one pupils per teacher against the optimum of twenty.

We have been relatively free of racial tensions in our public schools. All schools of course are integrated, both students and faculty. Some 70 percent of the enrollment is black; so is more than half of the professional staff. The school board has a continuing policy of seeking more qualified black teachers, but they are in short supply, making up only 10 percent of the nation's total.

St. Louis has been busing students for some years without fuss or feathers. Some 9,000 kids ride buses daily, not for purposes of integration, but to relieve overcrowding in ghetto schools. The city definitely needs more and newer schools. Half of the city's 150 schools are more than fifty years old, and 36 of them date back to the turn of the century.

Some years ago, St. Louis began to decentralize the school administration by taking key administrators out of downtown headquarters and spotting them closer to grass-roots sentiment. Five districts were established, each with its own superintendent. Three of the five are black. Each school district has a Parents Congress, at which fathers and mothers meet with the superintendent and principals. Official-public dialogue is frequent and productive.

In one respect St. Louis schools are as up-to-date as the next big-city system: Some of the kids smoke marijuana and there have been a few instances of hard-drug users. However, there have been few serious drug-related incidents, and both police and school officials are satisfied that dope pushers do not operate openly on school property.

The matter of juvenile drug addiction is one area in which our more-than-two-thirds-black schools of the central city have an advantage over the lily-white schools of well-heeled St. Louis County. The suburban schools have much more trouble with youthful addicts and pot smokers and for obvious reasons: Heroin is outrageously (but unfortunately not prohibitively) expensive; even marijuana costs more than the ghetto kids can afford. The suburban kids with a healthy weekly allowance find it easier to slip into unhealthy habits.

II

We persuade the underprivileged boy, usually black, to stay in school beyond the compulsory age (16 in Missouri), because, we say, the more education he has the easier it will be to find a job. With the national unemployment rate remaining stubbornly above 5 percent, the jobless black finds he has one-third less chance of filling an opening than a white youth. Will a high school diploma really improve his chances of getting a job?

Unfortunately, the answer to that question is too often seen by driving through the ghetto and counting the young people sitting on doorsteps or standing in front of the corner drugstore.

Thomas Purcell, St. Louis director for the Federal Emergency Employment program, had nearly 16,000 applications for the 980 jobs he had available in the area. But we do have other programs available to relieve some of the pressure on the tight job market, both in the public sector and the private.

One of the fastest-growing job markets in the country is that of local government employment. The national payroll of people working for state and city governments increased from 3.6 million in 1947 to nearly

10 million in 1970. R. Elliott Scearce, personnel director for the City of St. Louis, hires 8,800 persons over the year for jobs ranging from zookeeper to watchman at the Municipal Art Museum.

St. Louis is of course an equal-opportunity employer, and since I took office, the city has been forbidden by executive order to do business with any firm discriminating against minority groups. Under my administration there were far and away more blacks on the various boards and commissions that oversee policy and operations for the city. The first black judge that St. Louis ever had was my appointment—Judge Nathan Young.

I also got a better break for city employees on the lower end of the totem pole, most of whom also happened to be black. When I moved into City Hall, the beginning pay for the meanest municipal job was below the poverty level. By 1970 it had come up to $3,758 a year, no bonanza by any means, but a definite improvement.

My administration was also trying to get blacks into business on their own. The St. Louis Municipal Business Development Corporation, which had been dormant when I took office, was whipping up programs to encourage black ventures in entrepreneurship, as well as developing more jobs in disadvantaged areas of the city. In fact, I was fairly well pleased with what we'd been doing to give the black man a bigger, fairer slice of the economic pie.

It was something of an unpleasant surprise, therefore, when a group of Negro leaders of the Democratic party marched into my office one hot July morning in 1970 and accused me of racial discrimination in city government.

The charge was especially painful to me because those who made it were not a bunch of wild-eyed militants with fright-wigs. Practically every black officeholder in St. Louis was there, from Congressman William Clay to our Negro aldermen. All the party stalwarts were there too, men like Second Congressional District Chairman Leroy Tyus, who do the nitty-gritty political work at the ward level. Many of them had played important roles in my election.

As the morning wore on, tempers and temperatures rose. Charges flew back and forth like Ping-Pong balls. Ironically, the city departments they singled out for their most violent accusations of discrimination were the two areas with the highest percentages of black personnel: Parks, Recreation and Forestry with 63 percent, and Health and Hospitals with 68.

It wasn't long before I saw what the delegation was really out to get—the jobs of my two most controversial cabinet members. They wanted me to fire my acting Director of Health and Hospitals, Dr. Herbert Domke, and Director of Parks, Recreation and Forestry, Louis Buckowitz. It was hard for me to believe that my Afro-American friends were serious. Asking me to get rid of these men was like asking me to give up my right arm. Dr. Domke was my prize appointment. Not only had it taken a country-wide search to find him, but the deal to get him called for one of the toughest decisions in my political life: I had to give up smoking.

The St. Louis Department of Health and Hospitals has a budget of more than $20 million a year and rising, with skyrocketing medical costs and the shrinking tax dollar. To find a man skilled in the arts and science of healing who could also administer a system of that size was not easy. Men of that calibre are usually not available for the $21,830 our civil service scale allows per year. But we looked anyway.

My safari pursuing a potential health director included such able men as Dr. William H. Danforth, then vice-chancellor for medical affairs at Washington University, and now chancellor; Dr. Robert E. Felix, dean of St. Louis University Medical School; and Dr. Robert W. Kelley of Washington University Medical School. For months the chase had been futile, but one day Dr. Kelley came to City Hall with my friend Willard Levy, a businessman member of the safari. They had a possible candidate: Dr. Herbert Domke, a former health commissioner for St. Louis County who had gone to Pittsburgh to become health director for Allegheny county. There was one drawback: Dr. Domke knew the situation in St. Louis and was not overly enthusiastic about returning.

"However," said Willard Levy, "if Mayor Cervantes were to give a cocktail party where Dr. Domke could meet the outstanding members of the St. Louis medical profession and see how important they think he is. . . ."

Carmen, who has a flair for entertaining well and does it superbly, was more than willing. So the reception to seduce Dr. Domke was on.

During the evening we added a few fringe benefits—a car and a new house on the hospital grounds built to his specifications—to his base emoluments, and Dr. Domke was tempted.

I had always been a heavy smoker, and the anxiety of waiting for Dr. Domke's decision as the hours wore on had turned me into a chain smoker without my noticing it.

But Dr. Domke noticed.

"Tell you what," he said as he watched me light a fresh cigarette from the fag end of another, "if you'll quit smoking, Mr. Mayor, I'll take the job."

We shook on it, and a few weeks later at the swearing-in ceremony for the new boss of health and hospitals I was photographed putting out the last cigarette I have ever smoked. When the pictures appeared in the papers, I got a rebuking phone call from Jim Holland of the Mound City Tobacco Company, in which I have substantial holdings, chastising me for trying to kill our business.

In the ensuing years I lost my cigarette cough and gained weight. I also gained great respect for Dr. Domke and the way he was handling the job, not only medically but for the courage he had shown in wading into the political situation in our hospitals that had contributed to the defeat of my predecessor. It was the same situation that had brought this delegation of determined and angry black politicians to my office on this July morning nearly five years later.

We have two large city hospitals in St. Louis—gray and aging Starkloff Memorial on the near south side, and Homer G. Phillips Memorial, in the heart of the ghetto. Homer G., as it was familiarly called, could be considered a memorial to the defunct proposition that "separate but equal" should apply to treating the ailing body as well as nurturing the burgeoning mind. The black community had been keeping a watchful eye on Homer G. since the rumors began that it was about to be closed. It had always been a racially sensitive spot, and it loomed big in the complaints before me.

The black delegation argued that a black hospital in the black ghetto should be directed and staffed by blacks. Dr. Domke refused to compromise where skill, education, experience, and competence were concerned. If the best man for the job happened to be black, fine—but he was not going to bend over backward to hire incompetents just to achieve a black majority in the top staff positions. He was adamant about his right to judge ability independently of race, and since his decisions often involved matters of life or death, I was determined to back him. If we were to lose him for ethnic reasons, I would never get a professional of equal stature to replace him.

The case of Louis Buckowitz, my Parks, Recreation and Forestry director, was quite different. Politics had played a part in my appointment of Buckowitz, but he had been doing a fair job and I was reluctant to fire him just because he was white and Congressman Clay's brother, who was very competent, wanted his job. Irving Clay, the congressman's brother, was my commissioner of recreation and was locked in a bitter feud with Buckowitz. Here was a naked struggle for power, and some justified complaints were blurred, some pressing issues clouded, by the dust and smoke of battle.

Whichever way the fight came out, the real loser would be the mayor. I was bound to lose important support in either case. Louis Buckowitz controlled the Tenth Ward, home base of Jim Geisler, chairman of the Ways and Means Committee of the board of aldermen. For the curious and devious reasons of practical politics, in order to keep my leverage on the board, I could not afford to antagonize Geisler by dumping his patron Buckowitz. This was a problem I could not finesse. The blacks were laying it on the line. The spirit of compromise was not abroad in my office that morning. I could still try, though.

When Alderman Broussard asked, "Will you subscribe to the proposition that racial balance works best for the community?" I could honestly answer *yes.* I repeated what I had said earlier—that as mayor I had to act in the interest of the whole city, sometimes at the expense of certain groups that had given me crucial support, black as well as white, but that in the long run I believed strongly that a stable and successful society must be one that is fully integrated.

"What nonsense!"

This stunning remark came from Alderman Joseph W. B. Clark of the Fourth Ward. He went on to insist that the city was separated into two distinct communities, black and white, and that the black community could not afford to worry about the city as a whole. Black interest must be focused exclusively upon getting as many jobs and appointments as it could by applying all the power it could muster in the right places.

Clark had always been solidly against all my programs, but I had never regarded him as a hard-core militant. He had come up by orthodox political paths through the Fourth Ward Democratic organization run by the late Jack Dwyer, a white Irishman. As president of the local NAACP, he had long been opposed to the very separatism he was now preaching. This was the first time I had heard the most frightening conclusion of the Kerner Commission report—that America was moving toward two racially separated societies—so directly articulated in nose-to-nose confrontation.

To me this was a shocking moment. It grew more shocking when I asked if there was anybody in that room who would publicly question the validity of what Clark had just said. There was a deep silence as my gaze traveled from face to face. Not a single voice was raised to contradict or even qualify Clark's declaration of separatism. Alderman Clark was recently appointed as the director of Public Safety.

I knew that many of the beefs my fellow Democrats had laid on the table were based on reasonable expectations denied. I realized that these fundamentally moderate black leaders had to reconcile their public positions with the inflammatory rhetoric of the militants. I was aware that the shrill, uncompromising demands were bound to harden many white hearts, and that the equally shrill reaction was not going to be music to black ears. But I was still unprepared for what was a radical change in ground rules by which blacks and whites were to reconcile their differences.

We came to several amical agreements that morning, but I did not deliver the heads of Dr. Domke or Louis Buckowitz on a silver platter.

As my disgruntled black friends filed out of my office, I couldn't help thinking back twenty years when my Brother Lu took my by the hand and showed me that the true path to public service led to the common good, not to the good of just one segment of the city. I remembered, too, when I followed his advice and became a supporter of open accommodations in St. Louis, how my phone buzzed for days with anonymous voices calling Carmen and me "nigger lovers."

The inner satisfaction I got from having stood fast on my principles was in the end my only reward. Dr. Domke has gone on to a more important job as Director of Health for the State of Missouri. And Louis Buckowitz threw his active support to my opponent in the primary race for a third-term nomination.

III

The public sector has a definite part to play in the unemployment problem, despite the call for self-reliance in President Nixon's second inaugural address. Even if some of the programs administered in Washington are turned back to the states and cities, most of the money must still come from federal funds.

It has always been my contention, however, the answer to the question of unemployment is best given by the private sector. The role of private industry in the urban crisis is to do what only it can do: provide jobs. It can also train and employ the "unemployable." Moreover, it must operate on the principle which alone can keep our economy viable—the profit motive.

Private industry is not a welfare agency, and providing jobs is not a giveaway routine. Private industry must keep the glitter of gold dust in its eyes and still make a profit in a highly competitive, cutthroat, economic world. Furthermore, it is cheaper to give a man a job than to keep him on welfare. "Give a man a fish today and you will have to give him another tomorrow. Teach a man to fish today and he will take care of himself tomorrow."

Businessmen are not being asked to give away anything. They are being asked to invest their money and ingenuity in upgrading the employability of the disadvantaged. It is no small task to hire people from the bottom of the ghetto barrel, to help them make the transition from a street corner to a job. But it can be done, and it has been done profitably in St. Louis.

The McDonnell Douglas Corporation is hardly a fly-by-night outfit. It can absorb a $400 million order from American Airlines for twenty-five DC-10 passenger liners without dropping a rivet on the Air Force's Phantom jet fighters or NASA's space capsules. McDonnell Douglas employs nearly forty thousand in its St. Louis plant alone, half of them production workers.

Several years ago, James S. McDonnell, chairman of the corporation, motivated by the shortage of manpower and the growing number of "unemployables" in the inner city, decided to experiment with hiring the disadvantaged.

Since the aerospace and aircraft industry is so highly professionalized and technically sophisticated, integrating into it people with no mechanical or mathematical background was not a simple problem. Not only military fliers and astronauts depend on the accuracy and precision of McDonnell Douglas workmanship, but also the lives of thousands of daily air travelers, to say nothing of the company's reputation and several billion dollars' worth of flawless product. Still, McDonnell Douglas believed that the experiment with "unemployables" could be carried out without sacrificing the high-calibre workmanship that is its hallmark.

McDonnell invested $8 million over eighteen months to train 15,189 people—5,633 of them Negroes. All of them were unskilled, lacking even a high school diploma, but not always lacking a police record, yet they emerged from a seventeen-week course as workers who could hold their own on jobs requiring precision accuracy. As trainee-recruits they earned $66 a week. At the end of the course, the weekly stipend was $97.20.

In devising a curriculum for a work force from the central city, McDonnell had to contend with the following challenges:

—How to reduce a complex element to component parts so simple that any trainable individual could master one of them.

—How to design a training program that would enable the under-educated, inexperienced tyro to master that single element in a short training period of four months.

—How to expand the company's recruiting program to reach the central-city-neighborhood "unemployable."

—How to modify personnel testing so that it relates to the person who cannot respond to questions based on middle-class experience he has never had: How can anyone who has never filed an income tax return answer questions about Form 1040?

—How to provide the special supportive services necessary to large-scale hiring of the disadvantaged without disrupting standard personnel practices and procedures.

This last point represents a departure from old-fashioned corporate hiring practices. It acknowledges that there are human factors which enter into making a man a productive worker aside from his skill at operating a lathe or a drop hammer. Aside from the "buddy system," which is not peculiar to McDonnell, the details of the supportive services confirm the fact that output depends on the whole man, not just the talents displayed at his bench or on the assembly line during working hours, and that the behavioral sciences play as important a role in his work as do mechanical skills.

What McDonnell calls "supportive services" includes counseling the neophyte in whatever legal, marital, or economic problems may be bothering him; transportation to the plant for the first few weeks in the form of bus passes; extra supervision until the tyro knows the fundamentals of his job; workmen's compensation insurance which he almost surely never had before; and counseling on the personal side of interracial relations.

Hundreds of companies across the country are now doing what McDonnell first did successfully in St. Louis.

St. Louis has a number of other programs in which private enterprise cooperates with government agencies in a community-wide effort to reduce chronic unemployment in the urban jungle. Work Opportunities Unlimited (WOU) is the job-finding, job-making arm of a comprehensive manpower program funded jointly by federal agencies and local business firms. The Civic Progress organization, which is composed of twenty-three of our largest industries, withdrew from WOU to work independently toward the same goals, but the smaller firms find the WOU staff of twenty-eight useful in tapping the reservoir of "unemployables." Potential employers receive twenty-five dollars weekly in U.S. funds for up to twenty-six weeks to train welders, repairmen, assemblers, sales and accounting clerks, and data-processing operators.

In less than two years, the WOU staff placed nearly three thousand men and women in WOU-developed jobs with some twenty-four hundred companies. The staff also developed the "buddy system," in which a veteran worker is assigned to an "unemployable" to make him feel at home with his new fellows and to help him adjust to his new surroundings and the equipment he will use in his new job.

Among the other joint ventures in chasing down the elusive job in St. Louis are the local branch of the National Alliance of Businessmen, whose director, Thomas A. Carey, is senior vice-president of the Bank of St. Louis; and labor's Human Resources Development Institute, an AFL-CIO program of which the regional director, Charles Bradford, is also chairman of the Manpower Subsystem of our Challenge of the Seventies.

People like my old neighbors of the Fifteenth Ward in South St. Louis are apt to say that so much effort finding employment for the unemployables amounts to coddling the ignorant, ignoring the willing, and rewarding the lazy. They say we should reread the text of Nixon's second inaugural and note his emphasis on self-reliance, self-support, and self-sufficiency. I should reply that this is exactly what we are trying to do in St. Louis. We realize that the long view—the remoulding of rural patterns to urban models, the upgrading of education, the readjustment of values—cannot be attained overnight. Meanwhile it is difficult for a man to be self-reliant with a background of borderline literacy and vocational skills limited to picking cotton, hoeing corn, or washing dishes. It is not easy to be self-sufficient with a wife and kids to support in a subhuman rat-ridden slum, and most available jobs just out of reach of black hands. That the "unemployable" is eager to work can be illustrated by the fact that for the less than three thousand jobs offered by the Work Opportunity people, there were twenty-five thousand applications.

The job gap is being closed only inches at a time, but it is shrinking, however slowly, in St. Louis. And the fact that it is being closed by communal effort in which private enterprise plays an integral part is something the city can be proud of.

IX

Promoting the
Smokeless Industry

Courting the Tourist Dollar Spells More Jobs

There is one St. Louis industry that cannot move to the suburbs, taking jobs and taxes with it. Tourism, the smokeless industry, is deep-rooted but it needs and deserves nurturing. Tourists not only do not pour noxious smoke and sulfurous fumes into our atmosphere, but in a good year, tourism and conventions will pump upward of $150 million into the St. Louis economy. The dollars spent by tourists are quickly passed on to businesses other than hotels and restaurants to pay for the goods and services demanded by the transient population.

The tourist dollar circulates eight times in the community. Not only does most of the new money remain in the city, but each ten thousand dollars creates a new job. If we could attract another million tourists, ten thousand more of our unemployed would go to work. Attracting them was part of my program when I first ran for mayor. After all, I was eminently fitted for such a promotion project. I had learned the techniques of showmanship in Hollywood.

I put the program into operation the day I took office. My inauguration ball was an occasion for the formation of the St. Louis Ambassadors, a nonpartisan organization dedicated to promoting the industrial, cultural, and educational growth of the city. It started out as the "Flying Ambassadors," since most of its members were dynamic young businessmen more or less continuously airborne coast to coast or even abroad, but with their roots always firmly planted in St. Louis. I pictured them doing a selling job for their hometown while they were marketing their own wares from Phoenix to Philadelphia or from Dubuque to Dublin. The Ambassadors Ball has become an annual affair ever since.

The local press had a grand time laughing at my high-voltage booster tactics and turned their cartoonists loose on the idea that this twentieth century Cervantes was just as crazy as the creation of that other Cervantes—the sixteenth-century author, inventor of that mad, romantic Don Quixote de la Mancha who charged full tilt at windmills he took to be hostile giants. Regardless of their good-natured jibes, I and my Flying Ambassadors carried on our offensive, confident that we were not attacking windmills in St. Louis.

In addition to singing the praises of "Surprising St. Louis" on their travels, the Ambassadors have undertaken jobs of homework to make their city more attractive to visitors. When the St. Louis Symphony was in tight financial straits, they pledged $100,000 to keep one of the oldest orchestras in the country afloat. When a survey revealed that twenty-seven of the sixty-six fountains and statues in the city needed plastic surgery, they started the face-lifting.

When, early in my first term, I decided to try to bring the Spanish Pavilion from the 1964-65 World's Fair in New York to St. Louis, some of my fellow townsmen thought this particular bit of insanity was in some way the call of my ancestral blood. Actually, about the only Spanish words I know are "no hablo Español," which always arouses looks of incredulous surprise from hotel desk clerks in Spanish-speaking countries when they see me write Alfonso Juan Cervantes on the register.

Spain has nevertheless played a major part in the heritage of St. Louis, even though the city bears the name of a thirteenth-century French king. At the very moment Pierre Laclède and August Chouteau were setting up the fur-trading post which was to become St. Louis, French King Louis XIV was ceding the upper part of the Louisiana Territory—the western bank of the Mississippi to Spain and the east bank to Britain. The news did not reach French colonial officials in

New Orleans until October, 1764, and by that time the settlement had been chartered and named for King Louis IX.

Although the Spanish military did not take over the city until 1768, the British moved onto the opposite bank at once, and the French who lived there crossed the river, preferring to live with their fellow Latins in St. Louis.

In 1800, the Spanish ceded the Louisiana Territory back to France, but the Spanish continued to govern St. Louis until 1804, when President Thomas Jefferson completed the purchase of the territory from Napoleon. On March 4, 1804, three flags flew over St. Louis, then a town of about one thousand. Spain had never officially returned title to France, so the French flag was raised briefly after the Spanish colors were lowered. After a few hours, Captain Amos Stoddard of the U.S. Army hoisted the Stars and Stripes—for good.

During the thirty-six years of Spanish rule, St. Louis had grown to an importance that belied its size. Not only was it an important center for trappers and traders of both the Missouri and Mississippi rivers, but it had become the gateway to the West, now symbolized by the soaring Saarinen arch that rises a majestic 630 feet above the river bank. The city grew steadily, and by the end of the nineteenth century, St. Louis was the fourth largest city in the nation.

The community seemed to burst into full bloom shortly thereafter with the World's Fair of 1904, the centenary of the Louisiana Purchase. Almost immediately afterward, the city receded from the peak of her glory and became a sleepy, dowdy old dowager, dreaming of the past. She roused briefly, shook herself and preened to shine by reflected glory when a young air force captain named Charles A. Lindbergh flew a plane called *The Spirit of St. Louis* nonstop across the Atlantic to Paris. That, you will recall, was in 1927. After that she drowsed for another quarter-century.

The rebirth really began with a forward-looking, imaginative mayor who presided over the city during the depression doldrums of the 1930s: Bernard F. Dickmann. My mother had worked tirelessly for him, and I developed a great respect and admiration for his accomplishments. As mayor, Dickmann joined with Luther Ely Smith in his great vision of a national memorial on the riverfront to commemorate the

Louisiana Purchase. His political acumen put over a $7.5 million bond issue in 1935 to buy and clear forty blocks of downtown slums. It would take thirty years for his vision to materialize fully.

When I took office in 1965, St. Louis was in the midst of another late flowering. The graceful and breathtaking Gateway Arch was about to rise out of the ground. The Busch stadium, with its touch of architect Edward Durell Stone's genius, was off the design table and was getting ready for the fifty thousand fans of the Cardinals, both baseball and football.

The building boom of the fifties had given the business section a new and exciting look. The city was ready for a shot of razzle-dazzle.

The spark that fired my enthusiasm for the Spanish Pavilion was not the memory of Grandpa Cervantes from Barcelona, but a phone call from my old friend and business associate Harold Koplar. He had just returned from New York, had visited the fair in its closing days, and had been completely bowled over by the beauty of the Spanish Pavilion. He thought it belonged in St. Louis.

I was not immediately impressed. The Spanish Pavilion did, at first mention, seem indeed to be a windmill, and I didn't need to go to Flushing Meadow just for the tilting. Harold was greatly excited, however, and he was not only a man of impeccable taste, which I respect, but his enthusiasm was contagious. He convinced me that I should fly to New York with him and see for myself.

I fell in love with the pavilion at first sight. Even in the chill of a New York fall, its stark, clean lines gave off the sunny warmth of the Costa Brava. Although its spacious halls and chambers were empty, they conveyed a spirit of kindly hospitality that dissolved the mystery of their intriguing shadows. Even the smell was fascinating: the 350,000 Flemish pine blocks that made up the Moorish ceiling gave off a rich, exotic aroma. The great works of art that had graced the exhibit were crated and on their way back to Spain, but the sweeping ceramic and collage murals, the metal and wooden sculptures of the gates and jalousies, made the pavilion, in the words of John F. Canaday, *New York Times* art critic, "the best total work of art" in the whole fair.

The Spanish government would be happy to present the $10-million jewel to any responsible party who would dismantle it and take it away.

The decision had to be made by January 17, 1966, or the fair authorities would demolish the structure. I wanted to make an offer immediately, but there were questions that had to be answered first. What would it cost to move the pavilion a thousand miles and set it up again in St. Louis? Where would the money come from? How would St. Louisans react?

I would have competition in the bidding. Several New York groups were interested. So was the city of Mobile, Alabama, which wanted to build a Spanish square around the edifice. I would have to move fast if I wanted the pavilion to take a place in the burgeoning redevelopment of downtown St. Louis.

Gone are the days when a mayor had nothing to do but welcome visiting firemen, cut ribbons to open new bridges, kiss beauty-contest winners, and mend political fences. The catalyst in the rebuilding of the core centers of an urban metropolis today is the mayor. New ideas must germinate and grow to fruition in City Hall—imaginative, daring ideas.

It didn't take me long to find out how daring the idea of acquiring the Spanish Pavilion was going to make me. I had guessed that dismantling and moving the structure would cost about $400,000, but to make sure, I asked John Soult, one of the top contractors in St. Louis, to get a professional estimate. John was a friend of mine and I trusted him. He took a team of engineers to New York and I went along. After a thorough examination, John stood in front of the pavilion and shook his head. He didn't think the job could be done for less than $2 million. I flinched, although his estimate and mine had one thing in common: I didn't have the $400,000 either.

However, I went to Manhattan with Bill Costello, chairman of the St. Louis Ambassadors, and Josè Alvarez, the Spanish consul in St. Louis, to meet representatives of the Spanish government. My first experience in international negotiations ended with an option on the building contingent on our being able to guarantee $800,000 moving costs by November 1. It was already the last week in October. So all I had to do was find a million dollars and enough land in St. Louis to accommodate a building with 120,000 feet of floor space.

The first thing I did when I got home was to assure the board of aldermen that this brainstorm of mine was not going to cost the city a penny; I had never envisaged using tax money for the project. I wanted official approval, however, and I got it unanimously—but with reservations. The aldermen wanted to know what I was going to use the pavilion for. The only thing I was sure of at this point was that the pavilion was a thing of consummate beauty and was bound to attract tourists to St. Louis. Besides, it had restaurants that had won praise from both decorators and gastronomes. And its 850-seat theater was a jewel.

Second, I telephoned the Spanish embassy in Washington and wangled an extension until November 5.

Then I gave my attention to the little matter of raising the $800,000.

St. Louis had once raised several thousand dollars in pennies and nickels from school children to buy an elephant for the municipal zoo, but this was an elephant of another color. The Ambassadors subcommittee of professional advertising, public relations, and media men sent out 300,000 letters over my signature soliciting subscriptions in the $10-to-$100 range, but I knew that they would not produce nearly the amount we needed. I called a meeting of the city's representative bankers, business and professional men, and civil leaders to discuss not only feasibility and fund raising, but the question of a site. Then I went out on a still hunt for the jumbo contributions, armed only with my own determination and an approving editorial from the *Post-Dispatch.*

One of my first stops was Edgar Queeny, whose father had founded Monsanto chemicals in a small wooden building on the South Side at the turn of the century. He had named the company after his wife, Olga Monsanto, daughter of a Spanish engineer. Edgar was a rugged individualist, and I didn't expect him to be influenced by any sentimental consideration for his Spanish forbears. But apparently he caught my enthusiasm.

"Would $50,000 help?" he asked.

I assumed this was a rhetorical question. "Edgar, would you like to put that in writing?"

"Don't you trust me, Mayor?"

"You know better than that, Edgar. But showing your pledge around town would be a great help."

"Have you talked to Charlie Sommer yet?" Queeny asked.

Charles Sommer was then president of Monsanto. I had not yet approached him. Ed Queeny picked up the phone and put me on. I talked for five minutes and had another $50,000.

Charles Yalem, a philanthropist who never stopped looking for worthy causes, pledged $100,000. Stanley Goodman, president of Famous-Barr Stores, and the late Theodore Gamble of Pet, Inc., came through handsomely. Joe Griesedieck of Falstaff Brewing Corporation pledged $200,000 and we named the theater after the brewery. But it was the little contributions that delighted me most—the thousand dollars raised by the Girl Scouts and the more than 17,000 names on the $10 honor roll.

When option day arrived we had only $630,000 in pledges, but rather than ask for another extension I took a calculated risk. I wasn't sure where the rest of the money was coming from, and we didn't even have the site tied down, but luck was with me. We had a million dollars by the end of the year.

There were plenty of other problems beside the financial ones. The logistic complexities were staggering. We had to transport 4 million pieces overland from New York to St. Louis before we could begin putting them together. Furniture and detachable interior elements weighed 320,000 pounds. Four vans carried 160,000 pounds of floor tile, ceiling blocks and leather doors. Finally, it took more than one hundred trucks to haul 2,200 tons of structural steel and cement slabs. Volunteers found storage space for all this impedimenta during the reassembly process. Andy Frisella, head of our moving committee, donated 20,000 square feet. International Shoe provided 50,000 more.

When a study by Economic Research Associates of Los Angeles found the project "economically feasible and advantageous," the Civic Center Development people gave us a site in the Gateway Arch-Busch Stadium region for rental based on a percentage of the gross receipts. The ERA report projected a half-million-dollar annual surplus based on 2,250,000 visitors with gross revenue estimated as just under $7 million. The report envisaged amortization of a bank loan of only $1.2 million and we were going to need more money.

The old kit of promotional techniques was brought out. A screening of *Dr. Zhivago* at $50 a seat. Dinner in New York at $5,000 a couple with cocktails at the Spanish Pavilion and round-trip jet fare thrown in. Ninety-three affluent St. Louisans flew to partake of the solid-gold menu at the Four Seasons, enjoying 150 pounds of langouste caught in the Bay of Biscay that morning, filet of sole Cordoba, wines from Navarre, sherry from Jerez where it was invented, and brandy by that old master Pedro Domeq. I didn't dare ask whether queso Manchego cheese from La Mancha was served because my name was Cervantes.

At any rate I raised the banner of the City of St. Louis over the pavilion in the presence of such fellow citizens as August A. Busch, III, Stan the Man Musial, St. Louis restaurateur Joe Kemoll, who pronounced the menu impeccable even if it was the first $5,000 dinner he had ever tasted, and Harold Koplar, who had staked out our claim to the pavilion and would run the restaurant in it when it settled in St. Louis.

The Spanish ambassador and his wife, the Marques and Marquesa Merry del Val, came from Washington to act as hosts at the pavilion reception.

Despite the success, financial and promotional, of the Gran Fiesta de España, we were still several million dollars short of the capital we needed. Some of the banker members of our International Pavilion Foundation were beginning to lose their enthusiasm. We launched another drive, headed by John L. Wilson and Clarence Turley—downtown businessmen and civic leaders again. I rounded up Wilson, Preston Estep, Jim Hickock, and John Fox of the Mercantile Trust Co. and drove out to the McDonnell plant to have lunch with James A. McDonnell, the venerable chairman of the board, in the company cafeteria.

Mr. Mac opened our conversation with a hard-luck story. The recent merger with Douglas Aircraft, he said, was costing the corporation millions of dollars. He just happened to have with him the financial statement of the new joint enterprise—and my heart sank. I was on the verge of offering to pay for lunch when Mr. Mac excused himself and disappeared for twenty minutes. When he came back he announced that if the McDonnell Aerospace Foundation and the Personnel Charity Trust Fund would approve a donation of $75,000, he would match it with another $75,000.

Then Roy Tarter, boss man of the Carondelet Savings and Loan Co. of the South Side offered us a loan of $2 million, with another half-million if we needed it. It began to look as if we were out of the woods.

II

Then trouble arose from an unexpected quarter.

Standing in the courtyard of the pavilion at the New York fair there had been a statue of Queen Isabella who, according to what I had learned in school, had financed Christopher Columbus's voyages of discovery by pawning her jewels. That was about all I knew about Isabella, but I was due to learn a lot more very soon.

The Spanish government had given the original Isabella statue to the United States to be appropriately erected in front of the Organization of American States building in Washington. However, Manuel Ortuño, who had managed the pavilion in New York and was going to manage it during the opening period in St. Louis, promised us a duplicate. The enterprising Spanish newspaper *ABC* raised $5,000 by public subscription and the sculptor, José Luis Sanchez, set about casting another queen from the original mold.

I thought the presentation of the statue would be an excellent occasion to appeal for more funds, so we made a splash of Señor Ortuño's good news. But it turned out not to have been such a good idea after all.

On October 23, 1966, St. Louisans learned that they were to get a statue of Queen Isabella as a gift from the people of Madrid. Ten days later, an important gap in my education was filled. I learned that 1492 was also the year that Queen Isabella expelled the Jews from Spain.

On November 4, Rabbi Jerome Grollman of the United Hebrew Temple delivered a scathing sermon in which he declared:

> If the Spanish Pavilion is an insult to every freedom-loving citizen of St. Louis, then the statue of Queen Isabella is an outrage. For Isabella is the most vile, debased, odious monarch of all history. . . . Urged on by her personal confessor Torquemada, it was Isabella who instituted the horribly barbaric Inquisition, the Inquisition in which Marranos—Christians of Jewish origin—were brought to trial and charged with heresy. . . .

After reminding his congregation that Isabella had established Jewish ghettos in the 1480s, the rabbi went on to demolish the "romantic myth" that the Queen had pawned her jewels to finance Columbus. The voyages of discovery, said the rabbi, had been paid for with property confiscated from the Jews expelled by Isabella and with loans advanced under duress by Marrano bankers.

To say I was amazed and shocked was putting it mildly. The Spanish Pavilion project had been in the news for nearly a year and nobody had disinterred these sorry fifteenth-century pages of Spanish history until that moment. I became more and more concerned by the letters and phone calls that came to City Hall. Many of the big contributors to the pavilion fund were Jewish. In fact, my very good friend Harold Koplar, who first broached the idea of bringing the pavilion to St. Louis, was himself Jewish.

If I had offended Jewish voters, however unintentionally, I would be punished politically. And yet to refuse a gift paid for by the people of Madrid could very well produce a diplomatic incident. When Al Fleishman, an influential Jewish layman with important corporations as his public-relations clients, echoed Rabbi Grollman's sentiments, and Rabbi Nodel said amen, I realized I would have to do something to temper the rising winds. I called Washington and got through to Nicholas Katzenbach at the State Department.

The undersecretary of state was not amused by my predicament. Spain would indeed be deeply insulted if St. Louis tried to return Queen Isabella's statue, he said. The Department would consider it a great favor if the City of St. Louis did not louse up the amicable agreements on which American military bases in Spain depended. Please refrain from making nose-thumbing gestures at a friendly power.

The Spanish government, in fact, smelled a nefarious international conspiracy cooking, and saw Rabbi Grollman's sermon as evidence of a Zionist plot unfolding. The American ambassador was called to the Foreign Office in Madrid and reminded that Spain still controlled Arab communities in Africa where Israeli interests were concerned, and that if certain Jewish communities in America were bent on stirring up a sleeping dog still snoozing after five hundred years, Spain had a few contemporary hounds that might be awakened.

I had been in hot water before, but I don't think I had ever come so close to being scalded. It didn't help when Manuel Ortuño assured me that the Sephardic Jewish community of New York, who traced their ancestry to Spain, had come to the pavilion to applaud when their rabbi received a menorah made by Amadeo Gambino, Spain's ace metal worker.

It was nice to hear from Mel Dubinsky, a St. Louis businessman, that the chief rabbi of Madrid had told him that relations were improving between the Jews and the Catholics in the ecumenical spirit of Vatican II, and that the Spanish Jews had forgotten about Isabella after all these centuries. After all, it was the St. Louis rabbis that I had to placate.

I got Mel Dubinsky and Morris Shenker to arrange a meeting with the Rabbinical Association and its president Rabbi Joseph Rosenbloom. It was a long and frank session with all parties anxious to reach a just and painless solution to a painful problem. With good will on both sides, we were able to work out a compromise. The statue would be received in St. Louis without fanfare and quietly exhibited in an inconspicuous spot inside the Pavilion.

Anybody who believed the rumor once current that I was bucking for an appointment as ambassador to Spain must have laughed when he saw Queen Isabella sulking in her obscure corner.

III

The pavilion opened with a resounding bang on the evening of May 24, 1968. The VIP guests paid one thousand dollars each for the privilege of attending the grand opening, getting a first glimpse of the charming edifice, and sipping sangria while they tuned their hearts to the staccato stamp of the Flamenco dancers.

Next day, sixty thousand turned out for the formal dedication and to fall in love with the pavilion. By chance, Jose Ferrer was in town with the *Man of La Mancha* troupe. As he introduced me to the crowd he remarked on the curious coincidence of an actor playing the role of Cervantes to be sharing the stage with a mayor named Cervantes.

There were great days in the months that followed. The restaurant, equipped at a cost of some $300,000 by Harold Koplar, drew warm praise from gastronomes for the epicurean menus. The jewel-like theater saw performances by stars such as Hans Conreid, Virginia Graham, Pat O'Brien, Gig Young, Cathy Crosby, and Martha Raye. The

Spanish Pavilion was the incongruous terminus of the 1969 St. Patrick's Day parade, when the Irish marched through the unseasonable March snow and sleet to drink German beer in the Hispanic lobby.

As the busy and exciting months stretched toward the end of the first year, financial shadows were lengthening around the pavilion. St. Louis loved it. The postcards tourists wrote home about it were enthusiastic. But the burden of its debts in an ever-tightening money market was just too much to be overcome by mere enthusiasm. Even though more than 800,000 persons from all over the world came to see this beautiful edifice, it lacked the confidence and the additional funds from the downtown business community. The pavilion closed shortly before the first year was up.

Spectacular though it was, I must admit that the acquisition of the Spanish Pavilion for St. Louis was not my most brilliant coup. But I have no apologies. The pavilion is too beautiful, too exquisite an *objet d'art* to remain fallow for long. I am proud that it stands near the banks of the Mississippi today. The fact that most of my friends still speak to me while their money is locked up in the pavilion is evidence that they have not lost their faith. Harold Koplar, who stands to lose substantially, still believes in his own esthetic judgment.

So do I.

IV

The local cartoonists had stopped drawing Mayor Cervantes astride the nag Rosinante, his lance at the ready for any challenging windmills, by the time the Spanish Pavilion opened in a brief blaze of glory. It wasn't long, however, before their pens were at work depicting me as the Admiral of the Ocean Sea, feet planted firmly on the poop deck of the Santa Maria, one eye glued to a spyglass focused on the Gateway Arch. I had been taken with another terrific idea for attracting tourists to St. Louis, and it had a Spanish flavor also. The newspapers that had usually referred to me as Mayor A. J. Cervantes now pointedly called me Alfonso Juan Cervantes. My latest project for a tourist magnet was to moor a replica of the Santa Maria, Columbus's flagship, on the St. Louis riverfront.

The Santa Maria I had my eye on was another refugee from the New

York Fair. A man named Lawrence Vineburgh had commissioned the building of the caravel in Barcelona to the exact specifications of the original—a vessel eighty feet long with a twenty-five-foot beam and a mainmast eighty feet tall. The planks were cut from the forests of the Pyrenees. The ship was equipped with all the fifteenth-century gadgets that had served Columbus and his crew—old navigation instruments, wine casks, water barrels, cannons, the galley—and life-size mannequins representing the crew at work. It was just the thing to attract an extra 500,000 tourists annually, but Vineburgh wanted too much money for it.

Summer passed, and I had almost forgotten the Santa Maria. I had been busy with urban problems, and what spare time I had was devoted to Hubert Humphrey's presidential campaign. Late in December, 1968, however, I found a clipping from the *Washington Post* that had come to my desk from O. O. McCracken, executive vice-president of the Civic Center Development Corporation, which operates downtown projects such as the Busch Memorial Stadium.

From the clipping I gathered that Vineburgh had taken the Santa Maria to Washington and anchored her in the Potomac, but that she could not compete for the tourist trade with the Washington Monument, the Capitol and the Lincoln Memorial. She was up for sale at a bankruptcy auction in admiralty court. I asked Bob Duffe to get me an appointment with Preston Estep.

Pres Estep was a country lawyer from Taney County in the southern part of the state. He had come to St. Louis in 1945 and made himself into one of the real movers and shakers of the community. At the time of his tragic death in 1970, he was among other things, chairman of the boards of the Bank of St. Louis and the Transit Casualty Insurance Company. He was one of the most adroit handlers of politicians I had ever met, and a man of immense public spirit. He was also a man of imagination, and he saw what the Santa Maria might do for the city.

Pres agreed to back the project to the extent of $350,000.

The auction was set for January 3, 1969. When I heard that Laurance Rockefeller also wanted the boat for a vacation resort of his in the Virgin Islands, I decided to go to Washington myself to bid against him. Jack Murphy, my attorney, came along to watch the legal angles.

When the bidding opened at $305,000 the Rockefeller lawyers immediately jumped to $310,000. I came right back with $315,000. The bidding advanced by $5,000 jumps until my competitors bid $340,000. I saw Jack Murphy eyeing me uneasily from the other end of the table, and I could feel the nervous perspiration on the palms of my hands as I addressed the admiralty bench.

"I bid $345,000, Your Honor," I said.

Murphy came over to me, and as he bent down to whisper in my ear we both heard the Rockefeller lawyers bid $350,000—the limit of my resources.

"Fonse," Jack whispered, "I'm still your friend, but I'm no longer your lawyer from this minute forward. You have neither the money nor the authority to go any higher."

He returned to the other end of the table, sat down and stared straight ahead.

I bid $355,000.

The bidding resumed climbing by $5,000 steps.

Jack Murphy was no longer watching anything. He held his head in his hands as if he'd been mortally wounded.

I was mopping the perspiration from my brow when my competitors bid $370,000. This was certainly out of my range, but I did want that boat. I'd get the extra money somewhere.

I bid $375,000.

The Rockefeller lawyers jumped up in unison and ran from the room.

They did not return at once, and the judge's fingers drummed anxiously on the papers before him. He yawned. The minutes ticked by.

"Your Honor, the bid is $375,000," I called.

The judge stared at the empty chairs of the Rockefeller attorneys. We learned later that the lawyers were on the phone to New York. They had reached their limit and were seeking authority to bid higher.

"Sold," said the judge.

I found a phone booth in the hall outside the courtroom and called Pres Estep at his bank.

"Pres, congratulations! You own most of a boat."

"What do you mean, *most?*"

"I mean $350,000 worth of the Santa Maria."

"What percentage does that give me?" He didn't seem to appreciate my humor.

I told him. I also told him that I'd raise the extra $25,000. His reply explains why I loved the guy.

"Don't worry," he said. "If it's worth three and a half it's worth three and three-quarters. We'll take care of it."

It did look like a good investment that would wow the tourists, and a dozen of my friends agreed to take part of the financial burden off Estep's shoulders.

The caravel traveled to St. Louis in pieces. In February, 1969, the dismasted hulk itself was towed by two seagoing tugs down the Atlantic Coast into the Gulf of Mexico to New Orleans and up the Mississippi. The fourteen tons of internal gear was trucked across country from Washington.

The berth prepared for the caravel among the sidewheelers and showboats already drawing tourists to the riverfront was not ready yet, even after the time it took to reassemble the craft. The Santa Maria had to be tied up temporarily to the Becky Thatcher, a sternwheeler which had been converted into a popular riverfront restaurant. However, the opening went off well, the caravel drew good crowds and lived up to everyone's expectations—except those who thought the idea was crazy from the start.

The gaps in my knowledge of Spanish history had already gotten me into trouble with the pavilion. If I had studied the history of the voyages of Columbus more closely, I might have been a little more cautious in my enthusiasm for this new venture. It seems that just eleven weeks after Columbus had made his first landfall in the New World, his flagship had gone down in a storm off the coast of Haiti on Christmas Day, 1492. Although the Santa Maria had been on the bottom for nearly five centuries, salvage crews were still diving to look for its treasure.

One windy and threatening Sunday I was sitting in the elegant Toledo Room of the Spanish Pavilion having dinner. Every now and then I would glance out the window and watch the progress of the heavy storm that was blowing up. It was warm and cheerful inside, and I was enjoying the food and surroundings when I was called to the phone.

"Al," said a voice that I took at first to be that of a practical joker, "did you ever see the Santa Maria floating down the Mississippi?"

"No, of course not," I said. My flagship was not scheduled to maneuver.

"Well, she's floating down the Mississippi now," said the anonymous voice. "If you hurry down here now, you may see her go by."

It took only a few seconds to determine that this was not a practical joke. With the sudden rise of gale-force winds, the Becky Thatcher and the Santa Maria had broken loose from their moorings and were waltzing madly into the churning midstream, buffeted between the racing current and the howling wind. The ghost of Columbus's flagship and the namesake of Tom Sawyer's girl friend were engaged in a dance of death.

The hundred or so dinner guests aboard the Becky Thatcher who had come for a drop of nostalgia with their cocktails and a touch of the romantic past with their steaks suddenly found themselves embarked on the most terrifying ride of their lives. As the two craft careened drunkenly together in the turbulent stream, the shriek of the wind was matched by the screams of the diners on the Becky Thatcher.

Luck was with them, however, as they approached the great pylons supporting the MacArthur Bridge. By some miracle the runaways missed the pylons, but smashed into the Monsanto pipeline landings on the Illinois shore. The Santa Maria, flying the royal pennants of Isabella's Spain gallantly smacked into the plebian obstruction first, thereby cushioning the shock for the Becky Thatcher and her frightened diners. There were no serious casualties—except my boat.

As I went out next morning in a Coast Guard cutter to survey the wreckage, I could not help thinking of John F. Kennedy's remark when someone asked him how he became a war hero. "They sank my boat," Kennedy had said, referring to the PT-109 which he commanded when it was sunk by the Japanese in the South Pacific.

I was certainly not going to be a hero to my friends who had anted up twenty-five thousand dollars each to bring the Santa Maria to St. Louis. The caravel was a mess, under water up to higher parts of the deck where a mannequin sailor seemed to be looking for help. Her hull was badly gashed and her masts and rigging were all awry. Apparently the voodoo spell that had doomed the Santa Maria off the Haitian Coast had followed her doppleganger to the banks of the Mississippi.

No voodoo spell could stop that dynamic young businessman named Sam Fox, President of Diversified Industries, who had already performed yeoman service for the Spanish Pavilion. He took over the chore of salvaging the wreck and dramatically renovated the runaway craft.

V

Both the Pavilion and the Santa Maria spectaculars were examples of private enterprise going to the aid of the tourist trade for the general good of the city. However, the city of St. Louis had taken official action, too, in pursuit of the out-of-town dollar. One of the first acts of my administration was to levy a one percent sales tax on hotels and restaurants. This tax brings some $750,000 a year to the city coffers, money used to advertise the attractions of St. Louis nationwide to bring more transients to spend their money with us.

The appeal to the retail tourist trade had been working very well, but we had been losing the wholesale transient business—the big conventions that bring thousands of delegates at a time to those cities equipped with shiny, modern convention centers. So we hired the Governmental Research Institute to survey the situation. The institute projected that a convention center would attract an extra $85 million of transient money annually. This would create seven thousand new jobs and, through the earnings tax, sales tax, franchise tax, and other levies, would bring more than $2 million a year to the city treasury.

Shortly before I left office the voters authorized $25 million in bonds to build the center. It was our administration's goal to finish the center by January 1, 1976, so we didn't wait for the sale of the bonds or the completion of land purchases to set the architects to work. Gyo Obata of the St. Louis firm of Hellmuth, Obata and Kassabaum are working with two black architects, Charles K. Jankins and Charles E. Flemming of St. Louis and Beverly Hills. The Jankins-Flemming team planned the Martin Luther King, Jr., Hospital in Watts, California, and several Model City projects in St. Louis.

The new center will offer some 250,000 square feet of space with a banquet hall holding nearly three thousand people. A recreation area for use of nearby residents is also in the plans. The structure will rise in the DeSoto-Carr urban renewal area to replace ancient derelict buildings. Plans call for developing ten blocks of hotels, restaurants and stores east and west of the center, giving a visual uplift to the northern flank of downtown St. Louis, adding to the new look of what used to be not long ago a slum conglomeration of pawnshops, saloons, and poolhalls.

So in enhancing the face of the city, we will be creating new jobs in a clean industry, bringing new money to St. Louis, and expanding the tax base to the relief of the property taxpayers who have not fled to the suburbs.

X

The Rebirth of St. Louis "Almost"

East Bank or West—Where Does the Airport Grow?

In the decade before the Civil War, bickering between conflicting selfish interests cost St. Louis a chance to become the second city of the American continent. Today, in the 1970s, the same lack of team thinking may be spawning another imbroglio.

In 1860 the city boasted a population of more than 160,000—a good 50,000 more than Chicago. Four years earlier, the Baltimore & Ohio Railroad had pushed its lines from the East to the banks of the Mississippi at East. St. Louis, Illinois. Inasmuch as trains are not equipped with built-in flotation gear, freight and passengers had to be ferried across the river to St. Louis while the city fathers argued long and bitterly about building a bridge across the Father of Waters. Most of the opposition came from the bargemen, who were making fortunes by their tight control of traffic into the most important transportation center of the Middle West.

While the acrimonious argument about spanning the Mississippi went on endlessly, the rail interests in Chicago took action. When the steel tracks first crossed the river at Rock Island, the center of economic gravity began to shift north from St. Louis. By 1860 Illinois had nearly 3,000 miles of railways running; Missouri had 817. When the first transcontinental railway was finished in 1869, its trains roared through

Chicago, not St. Louis. By 1910 the population of Chicago was 2,200,000—more than triple that of St. Louis. St. Louis had definitely missed the express, and having missed it, went back to sleep.

A century later, the city risks missing the jet plane for the same reason—brawling too long and loudly instead of cooperating for the common good. Empty talk proved costly when the age of steam was reaching maturity; it may prove disastrous in the expanding age of air travel.

The city awoke briefly to the sound of airplane engines when Charles Lindbergh flew the *Spirit of St. Louis* to Paris in 1927. This bold venture by the shy, young airmail pilot was backed by St. Louis money and St. Louis vision.

It was vision of that kind that I wanted to emulate when I declared at my first inauguration that I intended to be the best mayor the city ever had—words which the *Post-Dispatch* called, with a not unkindly editorial smile, "engagingly brash." I meant them, though, and as a step toward their implementation, I began immediately to do some long-range planning for the airport needs of the area.

Before I became mayor there was a modicum of cooperation and coordination between city and county in mapping modern air-transport facilities, but during my first year in office (1965) the City-County Airport Commission was dissolved. The county council, in voting to withdraw, recommended the acquisition of a second airport, but indicated "its inability to provide substantial funds for airport site acquisition." So the city, which was sinking deeper into the financial mire day by day, was going to have to foot the bills for any new development.

Lambert Field, the current international airport, is situated deep in the county some ten miles beyond the city line. It is quite convenient for suburbanites, less so for city people. And while there had been talk about a second airport, nobody in state government had mentioned committing state money for the project. Neither had Missouri representatives in Washington shown any interest. Meanwhile, Chicago was handling two thousand flights a day, and our cross-state sister, Kansas City, was well along with the construction of her modern terminal. It was up to the City of St. Louis to move and move quickly, because planning and building an airport is not an overnight affair. Even with an early start, it would probably be 1980 before planes would be landing and taking off—and I would be long out of office by then.

It was January, 1967, before the consultants I had set to work reported that the city should begin at once assembling parcels of land if we intended to have a new airport ready by the time Lambert became impossible. I sat down with the airport commission to discuss the many sticky factors that surround choosing a feasible site. At least 18,000 acres would be needed for a modern terminal in an urban area, and it is not easy to find that much space where the factor of ready accessibility will not clash with the potential danger of damage to the environment. On the other hand, everyone who has paid the fat taxi fare to or from Dulles Airport in Washington or Kennedy in New York knows the importance of easy accessibility. There is also the factor of congested air space, as travelers who have wheeled dizzily in a holding pattern for an hour over Los Angeles or Chicago will testify.

So the quiet hunt for suitable terrain was begun—some preliminary secrecy was necessary to protect the city from land speculators, who inevitably run up prices whenever they smell a possible windfall. The objective, as outlined by the commission chairman: "The immediate need to acquire a site within the State of Missouri and within a radius of 30 miles from downtown St. Louis."

Although Federal Aviation Administration officials, who would have to approve the site, warned that the thirty-mile radius would include considerable territory across the Mississippi in Illinois, nobody on the commission—certainly not I—ever gave a thought to any site outside Missouri. The principal requisite for any location was that it should foster the interests of the citizens of St. Louis.

Meanwhile there was a pressing need to expand and improve the obsolescent plant at Lambert. A $200 million bond issue that I presented to assure the city first-rate air transport at the present site was passed overwhelmingly. This evident public interest was to me a clear mandate to go ahead quickly with plans for a brand-new terminal. I hired a firm of consulting engineers (Horner and Shifrin) to survey the metropolitan area and recommend a site that would meet the criteria of terrain, accessibility, environment, airspace clearance, and land cost.

The study was completed and presented to the city in August, 1969. When I read it I was flabbergasted. So was everyone else concerned.

The engineers had considered six sites in Missouri and six in Illinois, applying identical criteria to each. Their report declared unequivocally that the most favorable site was in Illinois.

The preferred Illinois location was only nineteen miles from the center of passenger origin, whereas the second and third choices were twenty-nine and thirty-eight miles respectively. And the Illinois site would require substantially less excavation than the runners-up.

Another disadvantage of the Missouri sites: they would drag the economic center of gravity even further from the already impoverished central city to the benefit of prospering suburbia. Despite my instinctive affinity for the west bank, I was not convinced that the best interests of the city would be served by building the airport in Missouri.

It seemed paradoxical that my jet-age determinations should flow from a tragic decision made nearly a hundred years ago by the city fathers of St. Louis. Back in 1876, the city decided to separate from St. Louis County. It was the county-courthouse politicians who wore the black hats in those days. The thriving city legislators drew a line at what they considered the farthest west the city would ever spread, and announced that henceforth the rest of the county would have to shift for itself governmentally. Thus, St. Louis is one of the few major cities in the nation not situated in a county. Both the impecunious city and the now-bustling suburban county were and are afflicted with long ingrown political and social factors that work to everybody's detriment, even though they work separately.

Because of this structural quirk, however, the mayor of St. Louis is able to deal directly with the governor of another state, and one day I found myself talking to Governor Otto Kerner of Illinois. It seems that Illinois had also done a study for a new major airport and the R. Dixon Speas Airport Consultants had come up with conclusions that closely matched our Horner-Shifrin report. Later, when Richard Ogilvie became governor, he asked me if I would be interested in discussing an east-bank airport if Illinois arranged to pick up the tab. I certainly was, but I managed to moderate my enthusiasm. I knew there would be political turbulence and downdrafts before I could sell such a scheme to the west bank of the Mississippi.

I took a lot of soundings, however. I polled the members of the airport commission. I asked the opinion of City Comptroller John Poelker, the man who later defeated me for a third-term nomination. All agreed that the city had an immediate and overwhelming interest in joining the Illinois project.

So the mayor of St. Louis opened immediate negotiations with the governor of Illinois. The state of Illinois was ready to raise the necessary $350 million to get the airport built. A new airport authority would be formed and would be truly metropolitan, embracing not only St. Louis city and county, but crossing state lines to the east bank. Ogilvie suggested the commission consist of eleven members, five appointed by the mayor of St. Louis, six by the governor of Illinois. At this I balked. Although there was little chance that I would do the appointing, I insisted that St. Louis and Illinois be equal partners, particularly as we would throw Lambert Field into the metropolitan setup to sweeten the pot. The city had to be an equal partner.

The major airlines liked the idea of the major airports being under the same authority, and it made good sense to the Federal Aviation Administration as well. But as soon as the written agreement was made public, a lot of people in Missouri outside the city of St. Louis found it made no sense at all. St. Louis County, although it had withdrawn from membership in the airport commission, now wanted in on the act. The county had a legitimate claim to a voice through the East-West Gateway Coordinating Council, which must okay all projects of a metropolitan nature, and County Supervisor Lawrence Roos chose the council to express his not-unexpected opposition. He spoke for suburbia but ignored my comment that it was rather late in the day for the county to be concerned in a matter for which it had previously expressed active noninterest.

Another previously noninterested party was the state of Missouri, which suddenly decided the question was too important to be decided by the city alone. In a chauvinist appeal to all good Missourians to come to the aid of the party and keep the proposed airport out of Illinois, Governor Hearnes asked the Missouri State Legislature to vote $100,000 for another feasibility study on airport sites on the *west* bank of the Mississippi.

It was interesting to note the alacrity with which the governor was ready to hand out $100,000 to duplicate the objective survey the city had made, in view of his refusal of my repeated attempts to get the state to help the city meet its crushing fiscal burdens. Even requests for funds to meet really urgent needs, such as dealing with teen-age hoodlums running wild in the streets, were met with the same answer: the state doesn't have the money.

But the state found money for a new airport study.

The state's survey proposal was immediately vetoed by the Federal Aviation Administration. The project, said the FAA, had already been studied to the point of exhaustion.

Opponents of the transpontine airport, however, were not-at-all exhausted. Some of organized labor was against me. Although airport construction and operation would generate upward of fifty thousand jobs and millions of dollars in wages, union dues paid by workers on the job in Illinois would go to locals on that side of the river. This fraternal business of hands across the river and all that was all very good as an idea, but the Missouri unions were not going to take the "loss of dues" lying down. This was not a happy turn of events for me, as I had always made a great effort to support the just claims of organized labor.

More opposition arose in an unexpected quarter. During his campaign for reelection in the summer of 1970, Senator Stuart Symington was asked for his position on the Illinois site. I had always been an admirer of the senator as a strong, articulate leader, whose decisions were based on an honest concern for the public good. I was sure his Missouri chauvinism would give way to reason when he had studied the matter and realized how necessary the new airport would be to the future of our central city.

Symington squeaked through with a statewide margin of only 33,000 votes over young Attorney General John Danforth. St. Louis city gave him a whopping majority of 50,000, which insured him the margin of victory. But if I was looking for a reciprocal show of warmth for the city, I was to be disappointed in his viewpoint.

I began to hear reports from quarters in Washington and from various opponents of the new airport that my enthusiasm for the Illinios site was based on personal interest; that I was engaged in land speculation in the area. (These rumors, of course, cannot be documented.) The exact area, as a matter of fact, had not been publicized; Governor Ogilvie and I had agreed that we would do our utmost to keep speculators from hiking land values. And, at about the same time, Senator Symington requested a copy of the Horner-Shifrin report, which pinpointed the recommended sites.

The senator did not get it then, but he did not give up trying.

II

Early in 1971, I received a four-page invitation to dinner. Beneath the imposing letterhead of United States Senator Stuart Symington was the breezy salutation: "Dear Al."

"On the evening of February 24," the letter began, "Governor Hearnes, Supervisor Roos, interested members of the House of Representatives, Senator Eagleton and I plan to meet with FAA Administrator John Shaffner in Washington to discuss the question of the new airport in Illinois."

The start seemed friendly enough, but the only one on the guest list who had been publicly sympathetic to my position was John Shaffner. In view of my refusal to honor Senator Symington's request for a copy of the Horner-Shifrin report, his letter smelled to me more like a summons to the Inquisition than an invitation to dinner.

The closing phrases were friendly enough: "Please let us know if you would like to join us. . . . If so, we would be glad to have you."

I knew it was imperative that my point of view be represented, and if he was planning to shoot it down, I would bring along my own team of marksmen.

My first choice was Howard Baer, long-time chairman of the airport commission, patron of the arts, a pillar of civic progress, and retired president of Aloe Corporation.

Second was John Fox, retired chairman of Mercantile Trust, largest of downtown St. Louis banks. Fox had served for years with the airport commission and knew the problems and economics of air transport.

As counsel, I retained former mayor Aloys P. Kaufmann, an aviation buff who, as president of the Chamber of Commerce after leaving City Hall, was vitally concerned with the development of St. Louis as a major air center. Kaufmann had been president of the board of aldermen and became mayor when his predecessor, William Dee Becker, was killed in a glider crash in 1944. Deeply dedicated to air safety, he was in the front row with facts and figures whenever an airport hearing was held. It was he who pointed out to me that out of the thirty-four hearings that had been held in the past two decades, Senator Symington had attended none.

Despite his lack of concern with commercial aviation in the past, the senator was·certainly trying to make up for lost time. He or members of his retinue pestered Bob Duffe, my chief of staff, trying to find out who was coming to Washington with me. Bob is very good at not knowing things. Apparently someone close to the senator had also gotten in touch with Howard Baer, because Baer called me apologetically to cancel out. I could understand his reluctance to antagonize Symington in public, for Baer was then engaged in a campaign to form a new tax district that would bring needed support to the city's zoo and art museum. Symington's influence in St. Louis County was formidable.

To replace Baer, I invited Erwin R. Breihan, executive vice-president of Horner and Shifrin, our airport consultants. He certainly qualified as an expert.

When Symington got wind of who was coming to dinner he raised the roof. What was the idea of trying to foist a Horner-Shifrin man on the party when we would not even let him see the Horner-Shifrin report? I then told Bob Duffe to furnish the two Missouri senators with confidential copies of the study. Symington still insisted that Breihan would not be allowed to speak at the Washington dinner unless we agreed to make the report public at the same time.

I decided to bring Breihan anyhow. The senator had a copy of the report. If he wanted to release it for the delectation of speculators, it was up to him.

Fifteen minutes after Breihan, Fox, Kaufman, and I had checked into our Washington hotel, my phone rang.

"How's Mayor Al?" asked a jovial voice.

"Fine, Stu," I said. "Nice of you to ask us. Are you feeling all right?"

"Who's us?" the senator asked, skipping further niceties. "I've got to know who you're bringing. Protocol, you know. Seating arrangements, place cards—that sort of thing. Who's with you?"

I told him.

"No, siree!" he declared. "This is a Symington party, not a Cervantes party. We've already read the Shifrin-Horner report. We don't need Breihan."

I told the senator I thought he would want the background on how the decisions were reached.

"Not at all," he said. "Your decision is made. I want Governor

Hearnes and Supervisor Roos to hear the other side. You can't bring Breihan."

"Senator, I'm bringing him. You can't keep us out."

"Well, he can't talk then."

When he sensed I was about to explode, Symington modified his gag rule. It would be all right if Breihan just advised *me* what to say.

I almost didn't get a chance to say anything at all.

The senator had set up a reception line at the elegant Metropolitan Club a few blocks from the White House. In addition to Senator Tom Eagleton and Governor Hearnes, there were all the congressional representatives from the St. Louis area, as well as County Supervisor Larry Roos, the only Republican. Also in line were General Elwood R. Quesada, first head of the FAA and a "St. Louisan by marriage"; his wife was the daughter of the late Joseph Pulitzer, founder of the *Post-Dispatch.* General William F. McKee, another ex-head of FAA, was there, and of course John H. Shaffner, the incumbent head.

While Symington was apologizing for serving fish instead of steak because February 24 was Ash Wednesday, Governor Hearnes whispered to me: "What's the difference? I'm paying for it."

I suspected that the "I" was a pronoun that stood for the state of Missouri.

We were not allowed to tarry over dinner. While the coffee was being poured, Senator Symington stood up and started reading a long, prepared statement that he was passing out. The ensuing discussion developed widely divergent views among the experts, who were almost unanimous only in their opposition to my position and in their opinion that St. Louis was lucky to have such a fine airport as Lambert.

Only Shaffner disagreed violently with the idea that Lambert was an adequate airport. It might do until 1980 when a new facility could be ready, he said, but it was hemmed in by surrounding communities and could not be easily expanded. He stood firmly behind FAA's interim approval of the Illinois site.

So much confidential information came to light during the discussion that I decided we might as well go ahead and release the Horner-Shifrin study. I stood up.

The senator kept on. "We want to hear from these other people. Lenore, what did you want to say?"

St. Louis Congresswoman Lenore Sullivan wanted to say that we should proceed cautiously and not waste any more federal millions on unfeasible projects.

I remained standing while she spoke.

"Bill," said Symington, nodding to Congressman William Hungate, "what have you to say?"

Hungate was from the exurbanite community of Troy and, not surprisingly, found the existing airport quite satisfactory.

I continued to stand. I ventured, "But Senator—"

"I'd like to call on Congressman Clay," said Symington.

William Clay represented the heart of the inner city. He was a tough, eloquent leader who spoke not only for black St. Louis but was one of the most effective voices in the Black Caucus of the House. On this occasion, however, he reserved judgment until he was sure what effect the Illinois site would have on his constituents.

I was still standing, but as Symington was bent on going through the entire congressional delegation, I started to sit down.

Al Kaufmann intercepted me. "Don't you dare sit down."

I stood through added remarks by Governor Hearnes and some new thoughts by Supervisor Roos. I was still standing when a slim hand went up and Senator Symington recognized his son James, congressman from suburban Clayton.

"I hate to take up any more of your time," Congressman Symington began.

"Take all the time you want, Jim," said the senator. "You haven't said a word all evening, son."

When the junior Symington was through, I was allowed the floor at last. My feet hurt as I cited some Horner-Shifrin figures in favor of the east-bank site—one of which was the comparative cost of travel from the center of passenger origin to the proposed airport in Illinois. The annual figure for the Illinois site came to $61 million, against $93 million for the closest Missouri site and $122 million for the second Missouri site thirty-eight miles distant.

A strong word of disbelief came loud and clear from the divan behind me where Governor Hearnes was reclining. I was startled, not because the expletive was unfamiliar, but because it did seem a little bizarre when uttered by the governor of Missouri in the presence of half the congressional delegation from his state.

I turned to remind the governor that he was mistaken in placing the origin of the figures; that they came from the Horner-Shifrin report.

The meeting was dragging into its fourth hour when Senator Eagleton got the FAA officials to agree to delay public hearings on the new airport for six months, a compromise I could live with.

Afterward Tom Eagleton came to my hotel room with the rest of the group from St. Louis city. He was pleased with himself for having made the only constructive suggestion in the whole emotional evening. I could fully understand and respect his desire to see the matter of economic impact on Missouri carefully analyzed. It was still not clear to me what motivated Symington's obsessive behavior.

It wasn't clear to Larry Roos either. We found ourselves in the same homebound plane and the county supervisor came down the aisle to talk to me.

"Al, you and I don't agree on many things," he said. "But I was embarrassed for the senator. I had no idea what kind of clambake he had arranged until he called us together at six o'clock for a dress rehearsal. I apologize."

When I got home I found a message of the same tenor from Congresswoman Sullivan's office.

There was no word from Senator Symington.

III

Two years later, the FAA still favored the Illinois site but had made no formal recommendation to the new Secretary of Transportation. One reason for the delay was the face-lifting of the Nixon administration. With the departure of able Transportation Secretary John A. Volpe, FAA Administrator John Shaffner was also on his way out and was understandably reluctant to commit his scheduled successor Alexander Butterfield.

Another reason was a sudden rejuvenation of opposition to the Illinois site, apparently prompted by my bid for a third-term nomination as Democratic candidate for mayor. The anti-Cervantes forces and

John Poelker, who had reversed his position, raised thirty thousand dollars from some source to buy television time extolling the advantages of Lambert Field. A huge jet was shown taking off gracefully and soaring off into the wild, blue yonder while the viewer was reminded that this was *his* airport—don't let anyone take it away.

Nevertheless, on March 6, 1973, the day on which I was defeated for the third-term nomination, the story that competed with the election returns for top position in the *Post-Dispatch* was headlined: "FAA REPORT FAVORS ILLINOIS AIRPORT SITE."

The report which was variously characterized as a backgrounder and an interim report (interim after two years?) definitely recommended the east-bank site in the Columbia-Waterloo area, Illinois.

The recommendation was immediately complicated by developments in Washington. Not only was there a new FAA administrator, but the confusion involved in the Watergate scandals spread to muddy the waters inundating the problem of the St. Louis airport. A senatorial assistant, quoted by *Time* magazine's White House correspondent Hugh Sidey when the Ervin Committee occupied prime television time, said: "We've been trying to get the St. Louis airport straightened out for months. . . . First John Ehrlichman had it, and he said he would make a decision. You know what happened to him. They told us the decision was in the hands of Egil Krogh, the new Undersecretary of Transportation. You know what happened to him too. Now there is a new Undersecretary. I can't even remember his name."

However, an analysis by the Economics Research Associates (ERA) leaves no room for doubt that the Illinois site is the answer to all but the most provincial arguments. Even the beefs of the labor leaders are answered.

Although there would certainly be a loss of some union dues to Missouri locals, the cause of the union member himself would be improved, says ERA. The ERA report assumed that the airport at Columbia-Waterloo would be under construction from 1974 to 1979. During this phase, ERA estimates that an average of nearly two thousand construction jobs would be created annually, with an aggregate annual income of $19.5 million! Half of these jobs would go to Missouri workers. In addition to the direct jobs, nearly one and one-half indirect jobs would be created for every one direct job during the construction period, for an aggregate income of $20.5 million. In all, the airport would furnish St. Louis with 40 percent more jobs per average year.

As for Congressman Clay's concern for his black constituents, the ERA report has this reassuring comment: "In 1970 . . . the growth of the region continues to be preponderantly in a westerly direction. . . . An eastern location would have a positive effect on the present urban core of the cities of St. Louis and East St. Louis. An eastern location would be a factor working toward a more balanced growth outward from the central core whereas a western location would tend to accelerate the trend toward the west and away from the urban core." In other words, the Illinois site would favor the inner city and downtown St. Louis over suburbia.

The Illinois site would also generate tax income for St. Louis, despite its location in another state. The city would benefit from sales taxes on retail, hotel, and airline business. The ERA report estimates additional annual tax receipts during the construction period (sales tax, income tax, and property tax) at $1 million for Missouri and $698,000 for Illinois.

Despite the overwhelming advantages to St. Louisans of the east side site, I cannot predict what the ultimate outcome will be. But I can predict that if the fight goes on while the years rush by, St. Louis will still be without an adequate airport in 1985.

Are we reliving the 1850s? The lack of bridges which cost us dearly in railway primacy has been remedied, but the Mississippi is still an apparent barrier to cooperative action and an invitation to selfish bickering. I am no longer mayor. My neck is no longer in the noose. But I can still wish that unselfish interest would prevail and forestall St. Louis from being grounded while the air age is soaring to new heights—and perhaps to Kansas City!

XI

The Cities Versus the Highway Trust

The Fight to Make Rapid Transit a Reality

The intergovernmental dogfights and selfish interests that have been crippling the wings of airport progress in St. Louis have, luckily, been less effective in the approach to urban problems of surface transport. While we could stand more cooperation between agencies in unjamming the monumental traffic mess, here again the chief opposition comes from conflicting selfish interests.

Characteristically, one of the factors involved both in creating the problem and in slowing its solution is again the movement to the suburbs. More and more suburbanites in more and more automobiles are driving to work in the city, where they contribute a small amount of taxes while blithely contributing clouds of carbon and nitrogen oxides to our already polluted atmosphere. If the nation's commuters continue to clog our expressways at the rate of half an acre of car for one driver, there will never be enough roads or parking space until the whole country is paved over.

The obvious answer to this phase of the problem is to provide adequate, convenient, and comfortable mass rapid transit. There will always be status-conscious snobs who will never entrust their persons to a bus or train, and they will probably survive any across-the-board solution. Nevertheless, if the number of private cars go on increasing in direct proportion to the rise in population—more than 112 million cars now jam the roads for 203 million Americans, one auto for every other man, woman and child—the other hundred million will have to take to the air or go underground with gas masks. However, there seems to be a gleam of sanity just over the horizon.

The St. Louis metropolitan area is not only divided between two states, but it comprises six counties and nearly 250 municipalities. During the 1950s, the area was served by fifteen private bus lines, some of which offered parallel service on the same streets, while leaving outlying communities with no service at all. There was no transfer privilege between systems, so double fares were common.

The fifteen systems were consolidated in 1963 under the Bi-State Development Agency of the Missouri-Illinois metropolitan district. The acquisition by Bi-State was financed by a bond issue of $25.5 million, of which nearly $7 million was spent in the first few years for 220 air-conditioned buses to replace badly run-down equipment.

However, the economic picture had blurred outlines. Bi-State's only source of income is the fare box, and this money cannot be used to provide matching funds for federal grants on a two-to-one basis for the purchase of equipment and facilities. Although some help could be expected on the local level, the body of financial aid must come from Washington.

Since the states now provide matching funds for highway construction, it would seem logical and fair that they do so for publicly owned transport. This claim is particularly valid in view of the imbalance that has long existed between expenditures on highways for private automobiles and expenditures for mass-transit systems. The St. Louis area transit system, for instance, represents an investment of $25 million, against a public investment of at least $750 million for the expressway —a ratio of thirty to one.

We in St. Louis believe we are entitled to a better deal, because we have come up with a solid approach to metropolitan planning. Our area is one of the most politically fragmented in the nation, yet we are united in the matter of taking a long-range look at what lies ahead in the field of surface transportation. During my first year as mayor of St. Louis, we formally established the East-West Coordinating Council, the first such agency in the nation created under the provisions of the Housing and Urban Development Act of 1965.

The coordinating council is a nonprofit organization, which draws its basic leadership from among elected officials from the disparate pieces of the jigsaw puzzle that make up the 3,567 square miles of the area. It is not a government and makes no attempt to be one. Rather, it is a medium through which counties and municipalities can jointly attack problems of area-wide interest. The area covers the city of St. Louis and the counties of St. Charles, Jefferson, and Monroe in Missouri; and in Illinois, St. Clair, Madison, and Monroe counties. The population of the region is currently more than 2 million, and 3 million is projected for 1980.

The council immediately saw the transportation situation as one of major importance, because the surface system, improved though it certainly is, will certainly be unable to cope with the population growth. Rather than improvise patchwork expedients year by year, the council set up an expensive four-year study of transport in relation to land use and development, commercial and industrial activity, traffic flow, and of course population growth. The general conclusion of the council-ordered study, not surprisingly, was that the development of a mass rapid-transit system was imperative before the decade of the eighties began.

A complementary study by the Bi-State Development Agency, using the council's survey for its basic data, has been proceeding in tandem with it, while zeroing in on the specifics of rapid transit. I have been very happy that this comprehensive farsighted approach has been made possible by interstate cooperation, in this case unhampered by crippling regional jealousies.

However, it is a long way from a survey to a functioning rapid-transit system, as the San Francisco Bay Area Rapid Transit people have found out. And the distance between conception and execution is too often measured in dollar signs. Unfortunately, the battle of the dollars is fought in Washington.

II

I say "unfortunately" for reasons that will appear later. The ultimate solution of the transport dilemma rightly belongs in the nation's capital. Cities are incapable of building and maintaining a transportation network alone. Railways, highways, and airports need federal help because they are of national concern. Even water transportation requires federal subsidy. The only trouble is that our absentee partners sometimes lose sight of the fact that the main purpose of a transportation system is a coordinated means of moving people and goods—not vehicles—from one place to another.

With all due modesty—which I admit is not one of my outstanding characteristics—I would like to point out that I was one of the first municipal leaders to indicate the direction in which the cities must head to prevent patternless, helter-skelter solutions of the transport problem. In the early years of my first term as mayor of St. Louis, I proposed a resolution to the Conference of American Mayors meeting in Honolulu, deploring the billions of dollars—not millions, billions— expended yearly in federal funds exclusively for the construction of high-speed highways across the nation, while the cities, with more than two-thirds the population, had to stand with hat in hand begging for mass-transit money. My resolution continued:

—Increased highway construction contributes to urban traffic congestion, leads to misuse of land, takes land off the tax rolls, and causes increased municipal costs for parking facilities, access streets, and ancillary services, and destroys neighborhoods.

—Serious deficiency in the provision of rapid-transit facilities can be relieved with federal assistance.

—A more proper mix of transportation methods must be devised to meet the needs of the nation's metropolitan areas.

—Therefore, 25 percent of the Highway Fund (no longer essential to the U.S. Highway Interstate system, now practically completed) should be put to work in the interest of the urban areas on the same basis that the U.S. government has been paving over the countryside: 10 percent local money against 90 percent of federal funds.

Why should the city—any city—need federal aid to build a rapid-transit system? I refer to the U.S. Department of Transportation for an answer. The minimum cost of a basic—i.e., barely adequate—urban transit system would be $28 to $34 billion by 1980. Since national fare-box revenue, still according to the Department of Transportation, cannot be expected to amount to more than $1 billion a year, the answer is obvious.

Railway Age for September 4, 1967, reported the high points of my proposal to the conference of mayors and, not surprisingly, smiled editorially upon an idea (which sooner or later and in some form or other is bound to take shape) that the future of rapid transit is going to depend upon the rails, not the concrete highway. Five years after reporting the Cervantes resolution, *Railway Age* published statistics in support of the proposition that, in spite of the highway lobby, mass transit will move on flanged steel wheels instead of rubber tires. The score card:

—The Bay Area Rapid Transit serving the San Francisco-Oakland-Berkeley-Alameda-Richmond metropolitan region is functioning and carrying thousands of passengers daily.

—The Lindenwold line from Philadelphia to southern New Jersey has been running since 1969 and is daily carrying 42,000 commuters, 17,000 of whom used to ride their own autos to and from work.

—Washington, D.C., Atlanta, and New York are digging new subways.

—Miami has voted funds for an elevated transit system that will carry 400,000 passengers a day in automated trains over nearly sixty miles of track.

—Buffalo and Baltimore both have new transit systems on the drawing board.

If we just stop and think, practically every major city in the world—whether it's London, Paris, Moscow, Berlin, or Cleveland—has mass rapid transit. St. Louis, like other cities of its size, should move forward with them.

Railway Age has pointed out that steel rails are not only cheaper than superhighways, but they are more efficient in moving people. Fast electric trains can move 40,000 people an hour, against 2,500 an hour for each lane of highway. And with less pollution. When the Chicago Transit Authority electrified the Skokie line, automobile travel dropped by 2,000 trips a day and airborne hydrocarbon pollution was 13 percent less along the right-of-way.

Governor Francis W. Sargent of Massachusetts sums up the situation succinctly when he says:

We found that we had defeated our own purpose and that we have been caught in a vicious cycle. More cars meant more highways, which meant more traffic jams—and the need for superhighways. The result today? Miles and miles of bumper to bumper traffic, creeping along hopelessly crowded highways. The side effect? Billions of dollars spent, more and more cities torn apart, more and more families uprooted and displaced. Worst of all—failure to solve the problem that started it all: how to get from one place to another.

The logic of all this seems so clear and indisputable that one easily wonders what all the shouting is about. Unfortunately—and this is a word I used in an early paragraph of this chapter—the influence of the dollar has raised its gilded head. The affluent highway lobby in Washington does not let such a little matter as logic stand in the way of its fight against legislation to divert money from the Highway Trust Fund for use by the cities to build and maintain rapid-transit systems.

The Highway Trust Fund was created by Congress in 1956 to finance the building of the interstate highway system which, when completed, will extend nearly 50,000 miles—the most comprehensive public works project in American history. The fund is fed by taxes on gasoline, tires, and trucking tonnage, which add up to about $6 billion a year. Under legislation on the books in the spring of 1973, the money cannot be used for anything but the building of roads, even though the vast interstate network (total cost: over $70 billion) is nearing completion.

The highway lobby is made. up of several organizations with the common aim of building more and bigger roads. The most influential is probably the American Association of State Highway Officials, which functions in every state. The association gets its message to governors and state politicos via engineers and contractors. The feedback gets to Washington in the form of campaign contributions and advice to senators and representatives.

The Committee for Action, composed of roadbuilding contractors, also hands out election-year campaign contributions to public works committeemen of both House and Senate. Members of the appropriations committees also get cash reminders that their votes are being hopefully watched.

Automobile clubs and oil companies also help support the highway lobby.

The highway lobbyists are so automotive-minded that they have on occasion tried to stymie construction of the Washington, D.C., subway and to divert a share of alcohol taxes into the Highway Trust Fund.

The favorite argument of the highway lobby is that the proceeds of the 4-cents-a-gallon tax on gasoline should be used only for the benefit of the motorists who pay it. This is a little like saying that the $10.50 tax collected on every gallon of distilled liquor should be used only to build sanitaria for alcoholics, hire doctors to treat their delirium tremens, and train personnel to rehabilitate them after they sober up and dry out.

The anti-transit lobbyists have recently run into opposition in the form of the Highway Action Coalition organized by John Kramer, a young Rhodes scholar from California. Kramer's declared objective is "to bust the highway trust," and he seems to have considerable moral support. A public opinion poll found a majority favoring a release of some highway tax money for use by the cities, and 54 percent would spend it on improving rail transit rather than air or bus lines.

The U.S. Senate voted in 1972 and again in 1973 to allow the cities to use their share of the Highway Trust Fund (an aggregate of $850 million a year) for improving their mass-transit systems instead of building more urban highways. On the first two occasions the bill died in the House, where congressmen from rural areas balked at helping move city slickers to and from their jobs rather than buying more roads to move crops to markets. However, when a compromise bill was resubmitted in the summer of 1973, the rural legislators apparently were convinced by public opinion and a realization that more than two-thirds of the nation's population live in cities. At any rate, enough congressmen changed their votes to allow cities to have access to the sacrosanct Highway Trust Fund.

The $23-billion highway bill that President Nixon signed in August, 1973, allows for the first time federal highway money to be used for nonhighway projects such as buses, trains, and other mass-transit facilities. It will not solve all transit problems, but it is an entering wedge. The bill provides:

1. On July 1, 1974, $200 million becomes available for municipal bus purchases.

2. In July of 1975, $800 million will go to cities for subways, rail systems, and buses.
3. The annual $800 million will be continued for three more fiscal years.
4. Cities in desperate need of immediate funds for mass-transit crises will be able to get federal grants by substituting their emergency programs for highway projects. Under the 1973 bill, an additional $3 billion is authorized for such urban needs.

This program is still some distance from the 25 percent federal subsidy of the Cervantes proposal, which I placed before the nation's mayors in the last decade. In any event, no matter how many buses or other rapid-transit vehicles St. Louis will be able to buy when the funds are finally released, they will have one advantage over the transportation of my youth: Americans will not be arbitrarily separated as they were on the sternwheelers *Saint Paul* and *J.S.*

XII

The Creeping
Tax Revolution

A Nationwide Mess Leaves the Cities Holding the Bag

A few months after the United States Constitution had been proclaimed in effect, Benjamin Franklin wrote to a friend: "Our Constitution is in actual operation; everything appears to promise that it will last; but in this world nothing is certain but death and taxes."

The Constitution, with minor repairs has indeed lasted for nearly two hundred years and promises to function for another century or so. But while the inevitability of death remains unquestioned, the matter of taxation is being reexamined and reargued with heat and intensity unequaled since the Stamp Act Congress of 1765. It is no surprise that the loudest arguments come from the cities, which, as usual, are getting the malodorous end of the stick.

Missouri has been in the forefront of the demand for tax justice. A year before President Nixon's first plea for national tax sharing, the Missouri Municipal League, representing 375 communities, adopted a resolution asking for tax sharing on a state level. The Nixon plea to Congress in 1969 for national tax sharing pointed out that while federal government revenues have increased ninety-fold in thirty-six years, the reverse is true at the local level, resulting in "a fiscal mismatch with potential Federal surpluses and local deficits." During the same period cited by the President, Missouri state revenues increased twenty times while the City of St. Louis revenues grew less than five-fold. At the beginning of the same thirty-six year period, the nation's cities furnished more than half of all the tax revenues collected by government at various levels. At the end of the same period, the cities accounted for only 7 percent of the aggregate tax take, while the federal government was collecting more than 90 percent.

This "fiscal mismatch," said the President, must be corrected by returning a percentage of federal resources to local government control and responsibility.

The cities have the right to demand a similar equalization from the states for the following reasons:

—Traditional taxes such as the property levy are grossly inadequate, particularly in view of inflation.

—The cities' taxing power is limited by state constitutions and statutes.

—Cities fail to get a fair return on taxes they contribute to the state.

—The state has an obligation to pay for those state services it requires of the cities.

—The state's tax effort does not match its high taxation potential.

This last point relates particularly to the state of Missouri. If Missouri would tax itself at the average level of the other forty-nine states, it would take a giant step toward solving the urban crisis on its doorstep. The living standard of its citizens would rise from the forty-first of the fifty states to the twenty-fifth, and there would still be a surplus in the state coffers. Missouri cities have already reached the limit of these constitutional, statutory, and economically competetive tax efforts. If only the state of Missouri would tax itself to the median level of its sister states, Missouri state income would rise by $129 million.

The urban tax problem is doubly complicated by that perennial *bête noir* of every big-city administration: flight to the suburbs. Not only does the city lose personal and corporation taxes that the migrating men and their factories take with them, but the return of certain other tax moneys to the city is based on population figures. Thus, when St. Louis lost some 128,000 citizens between the 1960 and 1970 censuses (from 750,026 to 622,236) the city also lost some million dollars in its share of gasoline taxes. Furthermore, the state rate for the earnings tax is based upon the population factor.

The balkanized pattern of local government in the two-state metropolitan area is no great help as far as St. Louis is concerned. St. Louis County alone has 95 separate municipalities, and in the Greater St. Louis area, 468 units of local government have taxing power. Restructuring the governmental functions of the area may be politically impossible, but ideally, all residents of the area would certainly benefit by a common approach to the problems of crime, air pollution, water service, and, of course, mass transit.

I have already pointed out the inequity in the school situation between city and county education, a nationwide condition in which the richer suburbs with a richer tax base can afford to spend more dollars per pupil than the impoverished inner cities. Since local property taxes are almost universally used to support public schools, the areas with the high property values inherently have more money to spend on education. The California Supreme Court found this situation unfair, a denial of equal protection under the law, and at odds with the California state constitution. Several other state courts made similar rulings. However, in March, 1973, the United States Supreme Court, by a 5-to-4 decision, found the property tax system not in violation of the U.S. Constitution.

In a case appealed from Texas courts, Mr. Justice Lewis Powell, a Nixon appointee, ruled that "education is not among the rights afforded explicit protection under our Constitution," adding his opinion that "where wealth is involved the Equal Protection Clause (of the 14th Amendment) does not require absolute equality or precisely equal advantages." A majority concurred.

However, all nine justices seemed to agree that the current system of financing schools, whatever its legal status, was pretty much of an outmoded muddle, but relief, five of them believed, must come from the state legislatures.

In any case, the property tax is obsolete not only as a means of financing education, but for other municipal purposes as well. In 1970 St. Louis voters rejected the property tax as a means of retiring bonds to build the new convention center mentioned in Chapter 9. Three years later, the same voters authorized the issuance of $25 million dollars in bonds to pay for the center with the proviso that the city use part of the proceeds from its Merchants and Manufacturers tax to retire the bonds.

The earnings tax, the sales tax, a share of state and federal taxes are absolutely essential to underwrite the more and more services that more and more people are demanding from City Hall. In addition to the usual police and fire protection, water and sewer services, streets and street lighting, parks and museums, health and hospitals, there are services that were practically unheard of two generations ago—services like the Municipal Legal Aid Bureau, the Housing Authority, the Metropolitan Youth Commission, the Citizens Service Bureau, the Neighborhood Beautification Commission, the Mayor's Office of Aging, and dozens more. They all cost money. And since operating the city at a deficit is prohibited by Missouri law, we had to ask our citizens to vote a sales tax in 1970.

Today the City of St. Louis spends nearly one-third of its budget for the benefit of the disadvantaged. The need for more police has almost doubled in the past dozen years or so, yet the Metropolitan Police Force has added only 2 percent to its personnel in that time. The need for more fire protection has not abated, yet we have been forced to consider phasing out some fire companies because of a need for economy brought on by the firemen themselves. The alternative would be higher taxes.

Taxes of any kind are never painless. Even at their most obviously essential, they inspire letters to newspaper editors ranging from grumbling to vitriolic. Yet voters are too often swayed more by an emotional appeal, particularly when it is orchestrated by a skillful public relations expert, than by sound fiscal realism. Take the case of the St. Louis firefighters.

In June, 1970, the St. Louis firefighters, through their Local 73 of the International Association of Firefighters (AFL-CIO), got the board of aldermen to pass a bill calling a special election to amend the charter to give firefighters pay parity with St. Louis policemen.

Now, I have always had a soft spot in my heart for firefighters everywhere. When I was a teen-ager exploring the continent, after my academic career had been terminated by request, riding the rods or thumbing my way with friendly motorists, I knew I could always find a place to sleep in a local firehouse. No fireman ever let an itinerant lad go hungry. And I love and admire the St. Louis firemen because they do an essential and hazardous job with skill and courage.

Nevertheless, on June 25, 1970, I sent the bill back to the board of aldermen with my veto.

The letter accompanying my veto summed up my reasons. First of all, I objected to calling a special election when the amendment could just as well have been submitted to the voters in the August primaries or the November general election. The $160,000 that a special election would cost could better be spent paving streets, fixing potholes or replacing obsolete street lights.

Second, and most important, giving the firefighters parity with the police removed fiscal control of the fire department from the city and gave it to state legislators from places like Chillicothe, Moberly, and Mexico, Missouri. As I mentioned earlier, pay and administration of the St. Louis police has been in state hands since the Civil War. It was and still is my belief that the city should have the authority to control its own fiscal affairs.

In the previous ten years, policemen had received eight substantial pay hikes, from a beginning rate of $4,365 to $7,363—an increase of 70 percent. Moreover, their fringe benefits were fatter than other city employees. A firefighter, for example, could retire at fifty-five with twenty-five years service and get half pay; other employees in a similar age and service category would get only 14½ percent of their retirement benefits.

While there is no doubt that the educational requirements for a good policeman are much more demanding than those of a firefighter, I pointed only to the more obvious disparities between the firemen's union proposal for equalizing ranks between the two departments. The union wanted a fire captain to rank (and be paid) equally with a police lieutenant. A police lieutenant supervises fifty-four men; a fire captain supervises four.

When word leaked out that I was going to veto the amendment proposal, City Hall saw the greatest invasion since the teachers, pupils, and parents descended on me to protest my delay in endorsing higher school taxes. The august aldermanic chambers had never felt such an ominous threat of violence since the near-riot on the day I first took my seat on the board twenty-one years earlier. A phalanx of uniformed firemen marched into the cupolaed hall on the day the aldermen were to receive my veto message.

Joseph McMahon, the effective and hard-working president of Local 73, let it be known that his troops were ready to strike if the aldermen allowed the mayor's veto to stand unchallenged. Although a strike by firemen was strictly illegal, the uniformed ranks made such alarming sounds in echoing their leader's threat that the aldermen were impressed.

The board overrode my veto by a vote of twenty-three to five.

The firemen's union hired Ed Finkelstein, a bright, young public relations man who had just set up his own office. He and McMahon organized a tight and turbulent $50,000 campaign to get the parity amendment passed. The firemen assessed themselves an extra $2.50 a month to pay off the bank loan that financed the campaign.

Ed Finkelstein wrote the "fact sheets" and organized the propoganda strategy. The smoke-eaters and their wives rang doorbells and distributed the tracts. The firemen themselves had time to devote to their cause because of the curious work schedule in force in the St. Louis department—twenty-four hours continuous duty at the firehouse followed by two days off. McMahon accused me of using scare tactics when I said we would probably have to reduce the number of fire companies and cut neighborhood services to find money enough to meet the payroll if the parity amendment was passed.

It was passed—by a vote of 44,055 to 24,309, just 4.5 percentage points above the required 60 percent.

Fewer than one-third of the city's 263,614 registered voters were concerned enough to go to the polls.

The firemen's victory celebration verged on the hysterical. Union boss McMahon led the crowing as a personal victory over Mayor Cervantes. Just as the campaign had been focused on me as the villain ("We'll bury that Spaniard," read one slogan), the official announcement of the voting results found the firemen's headquarters ready with previously printed placards reading "The Santa Maria Just Sank Again," "Who Says You Can't Beat City Hall?" and "McMahon for Mayor." Several hundred firemen waving beer cans, throwing confetti into passing cars, shaking hands with policemen, and putting their helmets on their wives' heads, marched gloating to City Hall.

City Hall, however, was dark. The mayor had gone home to ponder the lack of concern on the part of two-thirds of the electorate who had failed to vote, but who would be footing the bill.

There was no lack of concern on the part of the St. Louis Civil Service Commission, however. The commission found that the parity amendment undermined the merit system and was therefore unconstitutional. Regardless of the vote, the commission refused to pay the 1,100 firemen at the newly increased rates.

Local 73 sued in circuit court and won. The city appealed to the Missouri Supreme Court, which in April, 1970, held that the parity amendment was not unconstitutional.

The firemen repeated their demonstration of triumph, happily indifferent to the city's problem of finding another $1.7 million by cutting such high-priority neighborhood services as improved housing, demolition of derelict buildings, tree trimming, street cleaning, health center services, neighborhood recreation programs, trash collection, street repairs, removal of abandoned autos, etc. Comptroller John H. Poelker, who succeeded me as mayor, is still struggling with the problem.

II

While it is true that death is just as certain as it was in Ben Franklin's day, it has been considerably delayed. A child born in the United States in 1900 had an average life expectancy of 47.3 years; one born today can hope to reach a median age of more than 70.

According to the National Bureau of Health Statistics, more than 20 million Americans alive today are past seventy. Those oldsters who have inflation-proof nest eggs or wealthy descendants who do not hide them away in cut-rate and disreputable "nursing homes" are no problem to the city. But of the five or six million who live in poverty, the vast majority inhabit the inner city, even if recently more have been turning up in what statisticians call "the surburban ring."

Those who live in the City of St. Louis are of course the mayor's problem, even though the Mayor's Office of Aging does not depend upon the local taxpayer. Our program for the elderly has been funded by the Missouri Office of Aging under provisions of the Older Americans Act.

I have had a special family interest in the operation of the program. My mother was working full-time at a paying job when she was past eighty and still found the time and energy for volunteer work. And my Commissioner of Aging was my older brother Lu.

As I have said before, Lu—the Reverend Lucius F. Cervantes, S.J., Ph.D—is a man of many and versatile talents. During my first term as mayor, he was director of the Mayor's Council on Youth. During the beginning of my second term, he set up the Challenge of the Seventies and was director of both the St. Louis and Washington offices. On loan from St. Louis University, where he is a professor of anthropology and sociology, he drew no salary from the city for his first years. In order to keep him on my staff after his university leave expired, however, I put him on the payroll; he turned over his stipend to the university.

With six books on social theory and family problems to his credit, Lu was well equipped to deal with the problems of the senior citizen whatever his economic, social, or ethnic group. As cochairman, he enlisted the services of octogenarian George Reeve with the object of recruiting the less handicapped of his generation to help the truly unfortunate. For while the major need of the elderly poor is almost universally financial—particularly in Missouri, where the welfare checks are almost microscopic—the most challenging problem has been to reach the people who most need help.

A recent survey by the National Council on Aging indicated that while the Department of Agriculture was returning as surplus funds allocated to food programs, a majority of the needy poor were not availing themselves of government help. The council interviewed 44,000 senior citizens in twelve typical cities and found that 24,000 of them were either poor (less than two thousand dollars a year for a couple) or near poor (less than three thousand dollars). The council reported that only 28 percent of the poverty-level group had ever applied for surplus food or food stamps. Almost as surprising, about one in seven of the poverty-level group had never signed up for Medicare; the figure was one in four among the blacks in this group.

To help reach this "phantom factor" of the elderly poor, we opened a downtown center for senior citizens—VIP's we called them, to placate the old curmedgeons who go around cursing "those damned golden years"—just before Christmas in 1970. The center was one of several where the undernourished could get hot meals for little or nothing. But it was also a center for a search for the people who needed the services we could offer.

Some of the services were designed to keep the elderly whose health was marginal from becoming institutionalized. Medical and nursing services were provided to keep the elderly at home, except in cases of serious illness. Homemakers, professional and volunteer, help with shopping and housekeeping. Free legal advice is furnished to those unable to pay, even to the housebound. A minibus system offers transportation free. A meals-on-wheels service delivers nutritious meals to the homebound. Leisure-time and neighborhood activities are programmed.

I think that even more important than the material help that we tried to bring to the aging is our effort to dispel the evil specter that haunts declining years—loneliness and the feeling that nobody cares any longer.

Prior to the opening of the center, my brother Lu, who had previously organized two televised forums on public affairs, presented an eight-part series over KPLR-TV called "Don't Grow Old." Designed to attract attention to the Mayor's Program on Aging, it was in effect a replay in St. Louis of the Second White House Conference on Aging. It brought to St. Louis such national figures as Senator Thomas Eagleton, chairman of the Senate Subcommittee on Aging; John B. Martin, U.S. Commissioner on Aging; William R. Hutton, executive director of the National Council of Senior Citizens; Arthur Fleming, chairman of the White House Conference; and Hobart C. Jackson, chairman of the National Caucus on the Black Aged.

And in April, 1973, after months of haggling with the White House, Congress passed Missouri Senator Tom Eagleton's bill for money to aid the nation's elderly for another three years. Although the amount has been trimmed, it will still provide money for low-fare transportation, nutrition programs, homemaker assistance, and multipurpose centers for senior citizens.

Unfortunately, no legislation can abolish loneliness and the hopeless feeling of being abandoned. That depends on compassionate fellow citizens.

XIII

The Reluctant Bigamist

How to Be a Good Mayor and Still Keep Family Ties Intact

Somebody once said that it was hard to be a good mayor without being a bad husband, because a good mayor is not only in love with his job but should be married to it. If that is the case I guess I was theoretically a bigamist for eight years. While I tried to live up to my promise to be the best mayor St. Louis ever had, I tried just as hard to lead a normal—or fairly normal—family life.

One by one, four of our six children have moved out of our home, to follow a husband, go away to college, or to have his own apartment. Only Cory and Brett have not left the nest. But the family ties are still intact. Judy, our eldest, has returned from Texas with her husband and our first grandchild. Two of our older boys are still in St. Louis also, so Carmen can usually get most of the family together for dinner once or twice a week. For me the occasion has top priority.

My staff would cooperate in getting me home in time. Carmen would always phone at 6:30 in the evening to inquire about my schedule so she could adjust her timing for taking the roast from the oven. Bob Duffe, Ed Golterman, A. J. Wilson, or whichever staffer answered, looked to my desk for a cue. If not in the midst of an argument with labor leaders or at the start of a crisis that would take an hour to build to a climax, the answer would be, "He just left, Mrs. Cervantes."

This was Bill Jud's cue to hitch up the mayoral Cadillac that would get us to my home in Westmoreland Place in ten or fifteen minutes.

I have mentioned Bill Jud earlier as my chauffeur and official ear to the ground, but he was a great deal more than that. He has been official photographer, personal pilot, bodyguard, (he packs a .45 and is a crack shot), and investigator.

William F. Jud had two years at the University of Missouri before economics forced him to take a job in private industry. He quit his job as field engineer to make a full-time career of his hobby— photography—but found he had to moonlight as a cab driver to make ends meet. One night during my first campaign for the mayoralty, my regular photographer failed to show up at an important meeting. Someone mentioned the fact that I had a photographer driving a Laclede cab, so I had the radio despatcher send him over. Bill Jud had the pictures on my desk next morning. I took him along to City Hall when I was elected.

Bill always took a personal interest in keeping me from making Carmen a City Hall widow and my children part-time orphans. On a night when I was due home for dinner, if some ribbon-cutting cere- mony ran overtime or a nonstop introduction delayed my getting a speech off on time, Bill would get to the radiophone in the Cadillac and call Westmoreland Place. "We're running twenty-five minutes behind schedule," he would tell Carmen.

Carmen has performed miracles during our twenty-odd years together in public life. She has not only raised a good-size family, run a big household complicated by large-scale business and political enter- taining, but she has proved herself an able politician in her own right. She went through the tough apprenticeship of ringing doorbells and waiting on freezing street corners while I held forth in warm living rooms. She developed the tactical talents, the little details that win friends and elections, the essential skills that I possess only in a lesser degree. She remembers names, keeps track of aldermen and department heads as they come and go. She is on a first-name basis with all the wives and even keeps track of the kids as they grow up. And she keeps me on my toes with clippings she slips into my pockets with her suggestions about congratulating so-and-so who has just been promoted, had a child, or won an award.

An example of the way she works is the rescue of her husband from an inexcusable gaffe the night I was installed as president of the Missouri Municipal League. It was an occasion for which I wanted to put my best foot forward, as the league played an important part in my effort to get a fairer share of state revenues to help the cities. It has considerable political clout.

I had a speech of acceptance crammed with hard facts and far-reaching proposals researched and written by my office staff. It was a solid speech and went over very well. As I sat down to bask in the applause, the lights were darkened for the showing of a new film about St. Louis. Carmen reached over and tugged at my sleeve—to compliment me on the speech, I thought.

"Nice speech, Fonse," she said, "but don't you think you should have mentioned Jim Eagan?"

Of course I should have. James Eagan, the dynamic young mayor of suburban Florissant, was the retiring president of the league. Jim was an old friend of mine. He had fought for our revenue-sharing program when many other mayors went along with the state government's thinking. He had supported me for the league presidency, too, against candidates from the western part of the state. Even though my staff had omitted his name in writing the speech, I should have remembered.

When the lights came on again I managed to get back to the podium just before the band started to play for dancing. I called for a standing ovation for Jim Eagan's unselfish and productive year of service to the league and got an enthusiastic response.

Only Carmen knew that I hadn't really planned it that way.

II

Among the many delegations that stormed City Hall during my occupancy was a composite group of some eighty women representing the various local organizations affiliated with the women's liberation movement. They came equipped, as do all special-interest groups calling on the mayor, with standard bearers waving big propaganda placards before the cameras. The television stations had of course been alerted. Their spokesman—or should I say spokesperson?—was an extremely attractive and telegenic young lady probably chosen to give the lie to a widespread belief that anyone involved with women's lib was either a hag, a lesbian, or a sexless harridan. I needed no such visual argument, for I had served on the National Democratic Advisory Committee with the chic Gloria Steinem.

"Mr. Mayor," said the spokesperson defiantly while the TV cameras zeroed in, "we've come to find out where you stand on women's liberation."

The walking billboards crowded in closer to camera range and I eyed the slogans uneasily. Some of them would give any politican the heebie-jeebies—and have.

"That's a pretty broad question," I said. "Could you be more specific?"

"Do you approve of legalizing abortion on request, Mr. Mayor?" she demanded.

"Well," I hedged, "that depends."

"Depends on what?" she challenged. "Do you or do you not believe that a woman has the right to decide matters concerning her own body?"

"She certainly has a primary interest in any such decision," I said. Actually I am opposed to abortion in most cases, but I was not eager for a full-dress debate. Not only did I hesitate to arouse the anger of a militantly opinionated woman, but there was a large bloc of my constituents sympathetic to her point of view.

"And what about day-care centers, Mayor? You want a woman to have unlimited numbers of children, but are you against day-care centers where she can leave them while she's out working to help support them?"

As a matter of fact I am convinced that a child gets the best care from its mother, day or night, but I was spared the argument by the comely spokesperson's nonstop flow of questions without waiting for answers.

"If you men would only stop exploiting women and pay them a living wage they could hire someone to care for their offspring at home. Or don't you believe in equal pay for equal work?"

"I certainly do!" Here at last was something I could agree with wholeheartedly, and I started to do so at length when Ms. Woman's Lib came up with another question, this one on the subject of prostitution.

At this point, the corner of my eye caught sight of another large delegation of women parading down the length of my office, skirting the television cameras to approach me from the side opposite the first group. My uneasiness returned. With the arrival of reinforcements, I thought, I was completely outflanked. I was wrong. The leaders of the second group stepped right between me and my first interrogator.

"Listen, you," she said loudly, ignoring me and confronting the other woman directly. "You folks shouldn't be asking the state to take care of your kids."

"And why not?" asked Ms. Women's Lib, turning on her coldest hostile glare.

The two women seemed about to square off for a hair-pulling match when I tapped the newcomer on the shoulder and asked: "Do you mind telling me who *you* are?"

"We're all members of M-O-M," she said. And when I looked puzzled, she added: "We're opposed to women's lib."

Then she turned her back on me and began in earnest to attack her female adversary, pausing only to glance at the TV cameras. As angry voices grew shrill, I saw a chance to get off the hook for once in my life. I edged away from the argument, leaving more than 150 women to settle their differences before the cameras without interference from the mayor.

III

Carmen and I have never formally exchanged views on the women's lib movement or our respective evaluation of it. I know, however, that while she frowns on some of their aims, she is sympathetic to those which would improve the lot of the underdog.

We both agree that women have been exploited economically in the past and Carmen would be the last to deny that man—and not only male chauvinists—have kept women from advancing to positions of responsibility in both business and the professions. Women, both black and white, have had to be at least twice as good as their male counterparts to get to the top. However, Carmen is no militant feminist, no proponent of the cult of unisex. She believes that men and women have complementary roles in most phases of life and that while these are different, each is equally important to our society. She believes in a division of labor and a specialization of skills. She is confident—and so am I—that if she decided to master the necessary disciplines, she could occupy the executive suite as a top-drawer insurance underwriter or a successful subdivider and developer.

She has already shown herself to be a successful politician. Yet rather than go out on the hustings and repeat the routines she had mastered during our salad days twenty-odd years ago, she has progressed to the subtler advanced techniques of opening our home to the people who may influence other people, to allow the opinion makers on all levels to get to know the candidate as a person. Rather than march with the female chauvinists carrying the banner of liberation and petitions urging the ratification of the equal rights amendment, she finds she has plenty of room for action with the rights that women already have. She enjoys the hurly-burly, the excitement, the crowded calendar that a political life demands. She finds no need to search for an identity. She knows who she is.

So do I. She is a person of enormous competence and charm, with enough organizing ability to handle a complex household with enough left over to keep me in line. Carmen is my personal Emily Post when it comes to protocol, a feminine Dale Carnegie when it comes to making friends and influencing people, the youngest-looking, most winsome grandmother in North America, and with all that, a perfect hostess.

Carmen not only has a great talent for entertaining but she loves it. In our pantry at Westmoreland Place there are several shelves of cookbooks. At our country place at the Lake of the Ozarks she has a whole library of works devoted to the epicurean life in all languages and for all tastes. What's more, she has the courage and imagination to use them.

The only time I saw Carmen ready—or nearly ready—to throw in her lot with women's lib was during a trip we made to Spain early in my first term as mayor. It all goes back to the Spanish Pavilion. Since my critics were calling it the "Mayor's Castle in Spain," I responded eargerly to the suggestion that I go to Madrid myself and take title to the pavilion for the City of St. Louis from the Big Boss, General Francisco Franco himself. Carmen would go with me, of course, and since this was an occasion where old promotion-minded Cervantes saw a chance to get a little publicity mileage for the hometown, I took my friend and business associate Harold Koplar along. After all, he was the one who first suggested bringing the pavilion to St. Louis.

Carmen, meanwhile, was giving the question of a suitable wardrobe some careful thought. She was by no means overawed by the prospect of meeting El Caudillo. We had been invited to dinner at the White House, and she was at ease with men in high places. She was unfamiliar with European usage however, and wanted to be sure she was appropriately dressed at whatever hour the presentation ceremony was to take place. I'm not sure what masterpiece of *haute couture* she chose—I think it was a Balenciaga—because Carmen was unimpressed by labels; her own taste is impeccable.

Our jet had barely touched down at Madrid's Barajas airport, when I began to suspect that I had underestimated the publicity possibilities. The Minister of Information, Manuel Fraga Ibarne, was hoping our visit would take off some of the heat generated by the pavilion running $10 million over its budget at the New York fair. Despite the fact that the impetus of the Spanish presence had quadrupled Spanish exports to the United States in one year, and jumped them another 200 percent by the fair's end, the business of the budget threatened a cabinet crisis. Dr. Fraga expected the presence of an American mayor might be a symbol of how tourism was bringing Spain into the twentieth century at last. He rolled out the red carpet for us.

Dr. Fraga called a press conference at Madrid's International Press Club for the man named Cervantes who couldn't speak Spanish. He had an interpreter standing by to field the questions of more than one hundred journalists from all over Europe, Asia, Africa, and the Americas. St. Louis had not had such worldwide attention since Lindbergh flew the *Spirit of St. Louis* to Paris. Even the rampage of the Mississippi River in 1973 got less coverage.

The emissary who was arranging the interview with General Franco called at our hotel the day before to check on last-minute details. I had been informed that formal dress was required, so I had to rent a morning suit for the occasion. I informed the legate that everything was in order, and that Mrs. Cervantes, Mr. Koplar and I would be waiting in the lobby when the car called next morning.

The emissary's eyebrows rose. "The car will come for *you*, Mayor Cervantes," he said.

"But my wife Carmen is with me," I said.

There was an embarrassed pause. Then: "We are sorry, Mayor Cervantes. General Franco does not receive women."

I dreaded having to tell Carmen that she had brought her stunning outfit all for nothing because El Caudillo turned out to be an ungallant male chauvinist who did not receive women.

Harold Koplar came to my rescue by taking Carmen on a shopping tour while I climbed aboard the official car in my rented morning dress to be whisked off to El Pardo where the dictator had taken up residence in the royal summer palace.

The approach to the palace was over moorlands covered with broom and through a park green with thick groves of live oaks. The final stretch down the long avenue lined with horsemen in full military regalia was impressive indeed. The polished splendor of the audience hall seemed to dwarf El Caudillo himself as he sat quietly at his desk and greeted me with polite reserve. General Franco was a rather small, soft-spoken, mild-mannered man who answered my questions with a terse *yes* or *no* or sometimes a silent nod.

While the photographers were recording the scene I could not help noting the papers piled on the general's desk. They reminded me of old state Senator Mike Kenny, who kept his desk in downtown St. Louis permanently littered with all kinds of important-looking documents. After seeing the same papers in the same place every time I called, I began to suspect that they were props designed for photographic purposes only. General Franco's papers gave me the same impression, although I must admit they had been more thoroughly dusted than the old senator's.

General Franco presented me with a medal—the Royal Order of Isabella la Catolica, created early in the nineteenth century as a reward for deserving Spanish colonials. It was an appropriate award for the mayor of a city that had once been governed by the very Spanish colonials who were the first recipients. It was not a medal, however, that would enhance my standing with Rabbi Jerome Grollman's congregation back home.

The interview seemed to be proceeding so cordially that I decided to ask a favor of the general. His daughter the Marquesa de Villa Verde, a stunning, ultra-fashionable woman, had attended the opening of the Spanish pavilion in New York in 1965. I told the general it would be wonderful if his daughter would come to St. Louis as our guest and help rededicate the pavilion in its new location.

"A splendid idea," General Franco said. I beamed—until he added: "But I think you had better ask her."

Here was at least one decision that the Spanish dictator could not dictate. I would not go so far as to say he was afraid of his daughter, but at least he would not venture to give her orders. He recognized that she had a mind of her own.

This was a thought that Carmen would relish.

She was not quite ready to forgive Francisco Franco, however, for being a boorish male chauvinist, even when Dr. Frago took us to lunch next day at Madrid's famous Jockey Club, one of the world's great restaurants, where diplomats plot power shifts over old solera sherry.

The red carpet that was rolled out at Barajas Airport stretched all across Spain—through Alcala de Henares, where in 1547 that other Cervantes was born, Miguel, the real McCoy, and where his birthplace has survived the wreckers' ball now destroying too many landmarks in impatient American cities; through Cordoba with its Moorish atmosphere; through Seville; to the romantic Alhambra with its breath-taking beauty; to the Costa del Sol, Malaga, and Torremolinos. Everywhere it was state dinners,—a long way from the homely stoops of Juniata Street, a world away from the angry delegations of black politicians and women's lib.

But I knew that as soon as our jet let down on the city-owned runways of Lambert Airport, new decisions and new headaches would be waiting for me at City Hall.

XIV

Options at the Crossroads

A Need for A Marshall Plan for American Cities

When I announced my candidacy for the Democratic nomination as mayor of St. Louis for a third term, I received phone calls from all over the country. Some of my best friends thought I was crazy. One of them asked, "Why in heaven's name should anybody in his right mind want to be mayor of a big city these days when urban problems are growing faster than crabgrass in summer, when Washington is still playing footsie with suburbia, and an epidemic of amnesia is sweeping the state capitals as far as the fiscal needs of the inner cities are concerned?"

Looking at the box score, my cynical pal might seem to have a point. Many of the nation's big-city mayors have thrown in the sponge during the eight years I was in office. Take Jerry Cavanaugh of Detroit, for example, one of the men I considered first-rate urban executives. Jerry was young, dynamic, with an instinct for placing all the pieces of the metropolitan jigsaw puzzle correctly. He retired when most men would just be getting their second wind and start looking ahead to the prime of public life.

Or take Art Naftalin of Minneapolis, who acquired his professional polish from a distinguished predecessor, former mayor, former vice-president, Senator Hubert H. Humphrey. Art put in his years as a solid, hard-nosed, hard-driving executive with more than a little success; he didn't stand for reelection. Tom Corrigan quit his job as mayor of Denver in midterm. Both Joseph Barr of Pittsburgh and Ike Davis of Kansas City performed with distinction, but chose not to go for an encore. The mortality rate for mayors running for a third term is high.

There are exceptions, of course. Mayor Dick Daley of Chicago appears ready to go on forever, and John Lindsay had a chance to quit when the New York Republican party refused him the nomination for a second term. Instead, he chose to run on a Liberal ticket and was victor in a three-cornered race. As we know, he refused to try for the third term. But I don't agree with my cynical friend that the exceptions were necessarily psychotic.

My own reasons for wanting to run a third time were multiple. First of all, I am in love with my hometown and I have loved the job of running it. I had not, however, completed my three-point program I had set as my goal eight years previously. And I still loved the challenge of getting things done, of overcoming obstacles, and the pleasure of seeing a project take shape and mature. I thought perhaps that in four years more I might come closer to achieving my objectives. They were:

—The physical rebuilding of the city.

—Rebuilding the lives of the disadvantaged.

—Rebuilding the health of the public treasury by strengthening the the tax base—the city's private economy.

I cannot deny that the ego factor has been a strong element in my affinity for City Hall. By that I don't mean the questionable pleasure of facing television cameras several times a week or seeing my pictures in the newspapers cutting ribbons to open a bridge, dedicate a new school, or welcoming some VIP from Novosibirsk. It's fun being at the center of things, but that sort of thing ceases to tickle a man's vanity after a while. The satisfaction that comes from conceiving a new program, however, putting it into action, nursing it along, fighting off its enemies, and finally seeing it come to fruition—that is the real job of being mayor. To feel creatively responsible for accomplishing something that will improve the life of the city is the inner stimulus that has made me wake up in the morning with the elation of just being alive.

However, the Democratic voters at the primaries decided that eight years of Cervantes would do nicely for a while. Too many ward leaders believed that *Life's* mudslinging article had hurt me mortally. Not wanting to back a loser, they mustered the sons and daughters of the folks who had backed me through the past twenty years and sent them out ringing doorbells for my opponent.

Two hours after the polls closed I had lost by the slim margin of 5,200 votes. Carmen and I went over to congratulate my opponent, Comptroller John H. Poelker. For eight years, I told my downhearted supporters who gathered in my campaign headquarters, Poelker had been with me 100 percent and that now I was going to be with him 100 percent. Someone in the crowd asked: "Does that mean you're through with politics?"

"By no means," I replied. After twenty-four years in public life I was not going to quit after a temporary setback. I was only fifty-two years old, and politics was part of my life's blood. I loved the excitement, the rivalry, my relationship with hundreds of dedicated people, the give-and-take of the campaign. I liked persuading people, fencing with the press, lubricating unyielding situations. I enjoyed the inner satisfaction of making the right decision. Even the embarrassment of making a monumental boo-boo was something I learned to live with as part of the game.

I remembered one awkward instance that might have cost me the election as president of the board of aldermen. Raymond R. Tucker, my predecessor as mayor and the darling of the big-business establishment, had dreamed up a new charter that he said would streamline the city government of St. Louis. To present it to the voters, he organized a well-financed campaign masterminded by expensive and expert public relations talent. The charter would have eliminated fourteen or fifteen aldermen, reduced the size of districts, and done other things that pleased Mayor Tucker, big bankers and big business.

I was against the Tucker charter because I thought it shrank participation of St. Louis neighborhoods in their city government and also diminished the voice of the general public. To try to defeat the charter, I mustered a group of small businessmen, neighborhood politicians, and labor leaders. My ally was one Sid Zagri, a Teamsters Union representative in St. Louis and a lobbyist for labor legislation locally. Sid was a heavy-set, dynamic extrovert, an arrogant and articulate character with a great talent for irritating Mayor Tucker and the Establishment. I took him to see Frank Bick, Sr., then publisher of the *South Side Journal.*

Frank was a gray-haired fireball of sixty-eight who had long supported me, and whose paper later came to my defense at the time *Life* magazine was trying to save its own existence by destroying me. In the back office of the *Journal* Sid Zagri, Frank Bick, and I drank coffee and plotted the ways we might defeat Mayor Tucker's charter, despite the backing for the charter by the local press and the money men. We had little money for mailings and other voter appeals, but we had enthusiasm and conviction.

We won. The charter was defeated and decisively.

Not long afterward, I decided to run for president of the board of aldermen. My opponent was Alfred I. Harris, reputed to be the white-haired boy of the Bricklayers' Union, an anti-Tucker anti-Establishment character who was against everything the big-business community stood for. So the Establishment found itself leaning toward my candidacy as the lesser of two evils.

To launch my campaign properly, we arranged a luncheon at the swank Park Plaza Hotel for the upper echelons of finance, industry, the professions—and labor. I wanted to prove to the members of the Establishment that I was deserving of their support because I was really not a bad boy and was really one of them at heart, even if they had not accepted me as one born to the purple.

To create an appropriate atmosphere for a friendly luncheon that was to end in a plea for campaign funds, cocktails flowed freely—a little too freely as it turned out. When I finally managed to get the Establishment's monumental thirst under control, I steered a cross-section of St. Louis big-shotism to the head table, where Al Fleishman, public relations dynamo for August Busch, III, and his far-flung enterprises, sat as master of ceremonies. Also at the head table, I had placed Frank Bick and his son Frank, Jr., who has since taken over the *South Side Journal* and has done an outstanding job in building the circulation to a quarter-million. As the dessert plates were being cleared, Al introduced me and I told the guests all the things they wanted to hear: what a great mayor the professorial Tucker had turned out to be, and how St. Louis was becoming a national center of charm and culture with our Municipal Opera and the St. Louis Symphony. I never mentioned the ill-fated Tucker charter, naturally—a useless precaution.

I had no sooner sat down than Frank Bick popped up, obviously feeling no pain, to let our distinguished guests in on a little bit of unpublished local political history. His tongue still in high gear from the last martini, he told how he, Al Cervantes and that diabolic conspirator Sid Zagri of the Teamsters Union, had met secretly in the back room of the *South Side Journal* to plot the obliteration of the Tucker reform charter. Frank, Jr., tugged repeatedly at his father's coattails but Bick delightedly continued his detailed account of how Cervantes outmaneuvered the Establishment.

I felt myself growing smaller and smaller while my face got redder and redder. As I watched the smiles freeze on the faces of our distinguished guests when they realized they were getting a collective raspberry, I wanted to slip under the table.

When Bick finally sat down, a chill silence settled over the room. What was to have been an enthusiastic fund-raising party dissolved in disaster.

Riding back to his office, Frank Bick, Jr., read the riot act to his father for spilling the political beans all over Al Cervantes' immediate future. Hadn't he understood he was destroying the atmosphere of confidence Al was trying to instill in his invited guests? For the first time Bick Senior seemed to realize the enormity of his actions. He blinked at his son and shook his head. In a subdued voice he said: "I guess I peed in the quilt."

However, I was elected in spite of everything.

II

I must confess that I remember the triumphs of my career with greater pleasure than the bloopers. A mayor does enjoy the privilege of rubbing elbows with other mayors and the men who shape the destinies of states and nations. At top-level conferences, in national political meetings, and at the White House itself, I have exchanged views at the top level. And although Lyndon Baines Johnson had an unchallenged reputation as the Senate's champion back-slapper, I have a warm remembrance of the late president's clap on the shoulder to welcome me into an informal conversation he was having with Vice-President Humphrey.

Carmen and I were invited to the White House in March of 1968 for a state dinner the president was giving in honor of President Alfredo Stroessner of Paraguay. While the strings of the Marine Corps band played through dinner, Carmen was watching the proceedings with a hostess's eye. From the size of the helpings of roast duckling that Astronaut Neil Armstrong was heaping on his plate, she judged that he was preparing himself for the lean days of synthetic meals squeezed from toothpaste tubes that he would be eating on his historic first lunar landing. And she noted with satisfaction that two of the three wines served were from California—a cabernet sauvignon and a blanc de blanc champagne—just like most of the wines in the Cervantes cellar.

After dinner, while Carmen was chatting with Lady Bird, I joined the president and Vice-President Humphrey in discussing my favorite topic—urban problems. Johnson, who was justly proud of guessing what other people were thinking of, somehow got the idea that I was hankering to be named American ambassador to Spain. It may have been that the grand opening of the transplanted Spanish Pavilion in St. Louis, only weeks in the future, had suggested the thought to him. I had certainly made no overtures and therefore was not disappointed when the president announced that he had promised the Madrid embassy to Frank McKinney, Democratic national committeeman from Indiana.

"There are other ambassadorships open, Mayor," the President said, "but Frank's going to get this one."

"Don't give it a second thought, Mr. President," I told him—and I meant it. "I'm more than happy where I am. There's a lot of fun and satisfaction in rebuilding a city." The president seemed to be in such an expansive mood that I slipped in a commercial for the home team. "Of course," I added, "we could use more federal help. Right now we're having problems with our Model City program. . . ."

This was an occasion on which President Johnson had turned on all his charm, and he had plenty. In a warm and friendly mood, he quickly picked up the cue. No one understood urban problems better than Lyndon Johnson—unless it was his vice-president, ex-Mayor Humphrey. Between them, they had done more for the inner cities of the country than any two previous administrations. I had sympathetic and appreciative ears that night.

III

While getting my second wind before looking down the road ahead, I'd like to take a brief glance backward to see how much of my program I was able to carry out.

If anyone asked me what I considered my greatest accomplishment of my eight years in City Hall, I would say:

"I like to believe I have turned the city around. I think I have sold St. Louis on itself."

Nobody has even questioned my talents as a salesman. I had proved this to myself by achieving success in private business before I made the city my business. The *St. Louis Post-Dispatch,* not one of my greatest admirers, once called me "salesman extraordinaire."

Item: After the voters had rejected a $2-million bond issue to complete the great Gateway Arch, our administration persuaded them to reconsider; they changed their minds by more than the required two-thirds.

Item: In eight years, our administration persuaded our citizens to vote more than a quarter-*billion* dollars in bonds—$7 million for capital works (more than 250 miles of street, park, and alley lighting), improving juvenile detention facilities; $200 million for improving the old airport; $25 million for a new convention center.

Item: Our administration sold the taxpayers on the idea of taxing themselves an extra 1 percent sales levy to provide more anticrime services without bankrupting the city. The yes vote: 68 percent.

On occasion, I assumed the role of traveling salesman. I often took to the road to sell St. Louis to the federal government. My trips to Washington helped corral federal aid—not nearly enough, of course—for fighting what used to be called "the war on poverty." We lured funds for temporary jobs from the Labor Department, more money for urban renewal and Model City programs. When I left office there were three major urban renewal projects underway to wipe out more of the city's worst slums involving 175 city blocks (645 acres).

Private industry was sold on the idea of cooperating with government in developing more housing for the low- and middle-income families. When I left office, Laclede Town was already a going and growing concern, and the Ralston Purina project in LaSalle Park was getting off the ground.

My administration's encouragement helped the private construction industry average more than $100 million annually in new buildings over the last five years of my incumbency which has also helped cut down the unemployment figures.

The Mississippi riverfront, once a shabby collection of decrepit structures, has been brought to a new life of usefulness and beauty. With the Gateway Arch as its center, it has become a prestige location for office and apartment buildings. Soon another sternwheeler (the *Admiral Jones*), a generous gift from an Ohio industrialist, will grace our riverfront. The flow of business and industry to suburbia has not been stopped, but has been slowed. The state legislature has been persuaded to pass an enabling act permitting the establishment of the Planned Industrial Authority. The authority would attract new industry to the city and encourage expansion of present firms through tax-exampt bonds and low-interest loans to broaden the city's tax base. I reactivated the Municipal Business Development Commission for the same purpose.

We encouraged the board of aldermen to utilize the revised Missouri Urban Development Law to permit the city to declare blocks "blighted" for purposes of redevelopment and retain the current tax income from the property. The tax savings has encouraged new building downtown.

We have made only a dent in the local crime problem, but it is a big dent. The local crime rate has decreased faster than the national rate, and should continue to decrease, since I secured for the city a healthy chunk of federal anticrime funds. St. Louis is one of the eight cities to share in the $160-million national anticrime program.

The crime problem cannot be solved at the local level in eight years, however, because it must be attacked at the roots—and the root causes of crime are national and fundamental. The mass migration of rural and agricultural and—let's put it bluntly—peasant populations, both black and white, into an urban civilization faster than it can be absorbed poses a nationwide dilemma which cannot be resolved on the city level alone. One does not treat a systemic disorder with an aspirin tablet. One cannot cure cancer with a Band-Aid. The absorption by the urban body politic of the transfusion of an uneducated semiliterate peasantry is bound to produce an immunity reaction, just as the human body rejects extraneous tissue. But I am convinced that in the long run we will moderate the crime-motivating division of social levels, and while the solution is more complex than what seems to be my oversimplification here, it will ultimately work if we treat the roots: education, adjustment of cultures, elevation of the standard of living another notch or two above the poverty level.

This brings us, of course, to the failures in our public-housing projects, which I admit appear to outbalance our successes. But we did learn from our failures, and the projects germinating when I left City Hall are growing in the right direction. Whether or not there will be real progress depends to some extent again on national policy. As long as Washington curries favor with white suburbia and lets the inner city stew in its own unsavory juices, we will continue to foster hostile failures.

The same applies to the racial problem, with which both the foregoing are intertwined. St. Louis has been fortunate—and I do claim some credit for my administration—in escaping the violent outbreaks in the 1960s and early 1970s while other large American cities were burned and violated. We have not been perfect in our interracial relations, but we have tried hard and we have the administrative machinery such as the Human Relations Council to continue the progress against discrimination. We cannot force bigots by legislation to love their fellow Americans of alien birth or faith or different pigmentation, but at least we can guarantee that the minorities will not be denied employment because of the difference.

I take pride in the fact that the lot of our black citizens of St. Louis has improved, however little, during the eight years' administration of a man who, sixteen years before he became mayor, cast one of his first votes as alderman against open accommodations—a vote he soon regretted. I think I have made amends.

I like to remember some of the little things I did that I think helped make St. Louis a better place to live in, the things my critics used to laugh at. They made fun of my selling the city on optimism, on persuading the weather telecasters, for instance, to say "partly sunny" instead of "partly cloudy." But the upbeat spirit was contagious, and the city was caught up in a sort of community feeling that led to neighborhood participation in cleanup programs and beautification efforts. "Operation NEAT," for example, saw more than five thousand on neighborhood teams planting trees, a program to repair eighteen miles of sidewalks, cleaning up a thousand vacant lots, creating vest-pocket parks, removing two hundred tons of trash, and getting four thousand unsightly derelict autos off the streets.

I remember the little things with almost as much pleasure as I do the major accomplishments, like getting rid of acres of festering slums. They help round out the picture (my claim) that I have left the city a better place than when I first entered Room 200 at City Hall. The city got used to my promotion methods before the eight years were up. I wore proudly the epithet bestowed upon me by the *St. Louis Post-Dispatch*—"engagingly brash"—as long as it got results. I like to think I did.

IV

A few weeks after vacating City Hall I was appointed adjunct assistant professor of urban programs at St. Louis University. My predecessor as mayor, Raymond R. Tucker, before he died, occupied a similar chair of urbanology at Washington University not far away. Nevertheless, I don't see myself leaving politics permanently for the halls of learning. The professorial interval will be an invaluable breather. It will give me the leisure to digest my twenty-four years of public service, to assess my experience in municipal government, and to decide how, besides sharing it with my students, I had best put it to practical use.

One thing is certain. Although politics was originally an avocation while I was starting up the lower rungs of a successful business career— my holdings in the eleven corporations in which I own controlling interest were placed in trust while I was mayor--it has since become my chief concern. Year by year, I seem to have become a professional politician and I take pride in the fact. Politician is not a dirty word. Politics—the art of the possible, or the science of government, whatever you choose to call it—is an honorable profession. Despite the well-publicized secret vagaries of the 1972 presidential campaign, it is not necessary to engage in dirty pool to achieve political success.

I learned one of the key principles of success in practical politics during my graduation from grade school—the art of compromise. I wanted long pants for my graduation suit. My mother, reluctant to see her little boy grow up, insisted on short pants. We compromised on a two-pants suit, one of each so we both won. A man may compromise without compromising his principles. I don't mean that the end justifies the means—it never does—but in the give-and-take of practical politics, in order to make a worthy program work, it is sometimes necessary to give a little to get a lot.

Whatever skills I have acquired during my two terms as mayor in City Hall I hope to put to ultimate use in pursuit of a goal. I have become more and more convinced it is essential to good urban government: to make the voice of the city more audible in state and national affairs, particularly to secure for the cities a fairer share of their own tax moneys, to correct what President Nixon has called "a fiscal mismatch."

We have seen some progress on the national level with the beginning of federal revenue sharing, but this has been offset to some degree by the garroting of antipoverty programs and housing projects which directly affect the cities. And we still have the antiurban sentiment from representatives of rural areas in both Congress and the state legislatures. A dreary example: The U.S. Senate twice passed a bill to allow the cities to dip into the rich Federal Highway Trust Fund to build and maintain rapid mass-transit systems. On both occasions the measure was defeated in the House by the votes of a few congressmen from farm districts. Fortunately, we now have a foot in the door.

Since 70 percent of the people of the United States live in cities, I have always been chagrined by the excess influence exerted on urban affairs by state lawmakers from bucolic regions. Why should legislators from Twin Bridges or Pine Tree, Missouri, determine how much the taxpayers of the City of St. Louis should pay their policemen with their own tax money? The cities provide more than their share of tax money to the state. They should get a fair share in return.

Even if the state had every intention of being fair fiscally—which it rarely is because of the one-way thinking of the rural legislator—the cities would still get cards dealt from the bottom of the deck. For many state and federal programs, funds are allocated on the basis of population figures, and the U.S. Census Bureau admitted in the spring of 1973 that the population figures for 1970 are inaccurate. There are 1,880,000 black Americans, the bureau says, who were not counted and who therefore have no official existence. That figure represents 7.7 percent of the Negro population, against 1.9 percent of the white population who were missed by the census taker.

Since three of every five blacks in the nation live in cities, the statistical nonexistence of nearly two million citizens makes an appreciable difference not only in money due the cities but in apportioning seats in Congress. Hence several millions of Americans, black and white, are theoretically unpeople and without representation in Congress. Moreover, although the discrepancy has been discovered only a year after the census figures were totaled, there will be no correction in figures until the 1980 census—except by act of Congress.

There is really no excuse for such a glaring example of shortchanging the cities, inasmuch as almost the identical miscount occurred in the 1960 census. It was repeated a decade later for the same underlying reasons that caused the failure of the Pruitt-Igoe and other housing developments: there is a fundamental misunderstanding by the federal bureaucracy of the psychology and life-style of its clientele, an almost total lack of communication. Had there been more representation of minority groups on the planning level, procedures would have been different. Many census questionnaires were mailed out addressed simply to "Heads of Household," unnamed, in the manner of junk mail addressed to "Occupant." They probably ended up in the trash can, if they ever reached the addressee. Anyone familiar with the state of mailboxes (if any) in a ghetto dwelling would consider it a minor miracle that the questionnaire reached the destination at all unless delivered by hand.

It is eminently unjust to let the cities go shortchanged until the end of the decade. The "missing" citizens could be restored to city rolls by rule of thumb. Using the Census Bureau's own figures, Congress could automatically increase the population figures for the cities by 10 percent—8 for blacks, 2 for whites. The extra money for programs based on head count would be useful.

This is just another example of the crying need for cooperation on all levels of government in order to give voice to all levels of humanity where there differentiation is greatest—the city.

V

Looking back through the pages of this book (which means looking back over my public career to date), I wonder if I have not left a question in the mind of the reader. In view of the dire predictions made in my introduction and echoed throughout the book, how do I reconcile this note of alarm with my inherent optimism which I have tried to communicate to the city?

I did allow myself a gleam of hope when I questioned whether the Great American Dream would turn into the Great American Nightmare before the two Americas learned to live amicably with one another. We still have a long way to go before the potential danger is past. The war for America's soul will not be over until the well-heeled and the down-at-the-heel, the prosperous whites of suburbia and the seedy disadvantaged of the inner city—largely but not entirely black—stop eyeing each other with hostile suspicion. But at least they are still talking to one another, and as long as communication does not break down entirely, I can hope that reason may somehow prevail over naked emotion.

The 1970s have started off in relative quiet. We have seen no widespread repetition of the raw violence of the 1960s. There has so far been no replay of Watts or Detroit or Newark. The Washington riots that devastated those blocks near the White House are a bitter memory. The mass charges against the war protesters have been dropped and the peace marchers have gone back to their classes. Los Angeles has a black mayor.

However, the relegation of some civil rights enforcement to the back burner, the curtailment of national programs designed to help the disadvantaged, and the general change in social philosophy in Washington during the second Nixon administration does not augur well for the mid-70s. The storm warnings may be going up once more.

Nevertheless my persistent optimism refuses to see nothing but black clouds ahead. The winds of change which have been blowing fairly steadily since the Franklin Roosevelt era have been gaining strength in the intervening forty years. We may have struck a lull, but it is not necessarily the lull before the storm.

One day the winds of change must blow free.